PRAISE FOR *THE WONDER WALL*

"I love this book. I am a huge fan of storytelling. And this book is one great story blended with cutting-edge academic work in the field of human mind and creativity. In *The Wonder Wall* Peter Gamwell and Jane Daly bring together decades of firsthand experience in creativity, leadership, and learning that I indeed will, as the authors suggest, read twice. I would urge you to do the same if you want to be in the frontline of finding ways to improve your schools."

—Pasi Sahlberg, Author
Finnish Lessons 2.0:
What Can the World Learn from
Educational Change in Finland?

"Take everything you know about learning and turn it upside down. It is there that you will find Peter Gamwell, Jane Daly, and their Wonder Wall of creativity wallowing in wisdom. Yes, we have three imperatives and four conditions, and therein you will find a treasure trove of ideas for creativity. You don't have to leave the school system to upend it. Just read *Wonder Wall* and you will be swept along into doing things that engage all students and teachers. You will even get ideas about how to evaluate creativity. The timing is perfect. Go beyond skills and knowledge, and light the sparks that lead to learning. Be excited about the limitless possibilities of education."

—Michael Fullan, Professor Emeritus
Ontario Institute for Studies in Education
University of Toronto

"Be brilliant at what you're best at. Build on your strengths. Belong to something. These are the three imperatives that this great book sets out for young people and those who teach them. It does so with wit, wisdom, up-close experience, and a magnificent capacity to tell a good tale of why all people in schools really matter. This book is its own Wonder Wall. When you've closed your Ken Robinson book, open this next. You'll not be disappointed."

—Andy Hargreaves, Brennan Chair in Education
Boston College
Boston, MA

"Peter Gamwell and Jane Daly have written an alternative manifesto for boldness, innovation, and risk in education. They do so with respect and regard for the enormous expectations communities already place on educators. This is an essential read that holds a code as the global community commits to attain the UN's Sustainable Development Goal #4: 'Quality Education for All.'"

—**Kathryn White**
President and CEO | Présidente et directrice générale
United Nations Association in Canada |
Association canadienne pour les Nations Unies

"We are preparing our children for a world that does not exist; where the pace of change is mandatory but growth only optional; where, Freidman argues, creativity, ingenuity, portability, and flexibility are the keys to survival. So, at last, a book which stands courageous at the crossroads where creative theory and practice meet; that Shangri-La where innovation and imagination thrive. Packed with suggestions and practical ideas, it draws a map for all those who believe there is always a better way. It gives leaders the confidence and the strategies to develop those conditions in which individual and group potential can be released. A must-read for all threshold adventurers. I have only one criticism—I wish I'd written it."

—**Sir John Jones, Author**
The Magic-Weaving Business
United Kingdom

"All of my life I have been enthused by two things: creativity and simplicity. I'm proud that I got in on the creativity thing before it became uber trendy amongst adults. It's always been at the heart of our children's agenda. As time has gone by, I have become increasingly concerned that something as primal and elegantly human as creativity has been stripped of its simplicity by so many, and as a result, turned into something almost mystical and increasingly complex. That's why, from the day I first met Peter Gamwell, I knew we'd get on. First, because he got it long before I did and second, because he is one of the gifted few who can strip back the nonsense and help us all to rediscover the joy of our natural creative state. This book is Peter bottled; I love it!"

—**Richard Gerver, Author**
Change: Learn to Love It,
Learn to Lead It
United Kingdom

"*The Wonder Wall* focuses on tapping into the creativity within ourselves to instill fundamental changes in the way people lead organizations and schools. Peter and Jane capture the pragmatic ways in which creativity and innovation can be stimulated and harnessed by bringing the best out of people in every sort of organization. This book isn't just another bag of tricks for managing organizational change. It is a heartfelt, deeply grounded manifesto for the more visionary and creative styles of servant leadership."

—Sir Ken Robinson, Author/Consultant
The Element: How Finding Your
Passion Changes Everything
Los Angeles, CA

"Peter Gamwell understands creativity like few people on this planet, and now, thanks to this stirring, entertaining, and illuminating book, we'll all understand it much more. If you're at all concerned with making the extraordinary happen in your organization, you need to read *The Wonder Wall*."

—Lou Aronica, *New York Times* Bestselling Author
Stamford, CT

"Effective and memorable anecdotes will stay in the reader's mind long after the conclusion of the book. The book acknowledges the drive toward innovative and transformative practices and provides a framework to foster creativity in complex organizations. A strong theory of action, the text highlights creativity, structure, change, and inclusive practices."

—Jill Gildea, Superintendent
Fremont School District 79
Mundelein, IL

"This important book lays out a journey leading to improvement that is strengths-based, and focuses on talent and inclusivity, with the outcome of a creative, innovative, and engaged organization. For engaging students in school, this book is essential."

—Lynn Lisy-Macan, Visiting Assistant Professor
University at Albany–SUNY
Albany, NY

"This book will inspire educators who may be stuck in their current context and encourage them to think out of the box."

—Karen L Tichy, Assistant Professor
of Educational Leadership
Saint Louis University, School of Education
St Louis, MO

"The authors present a compelling and refreshing narrative that transcends much of the pedestrian nature of education dialogue. The focus on learning is wonderful."

—Peter Dillon, Superintendent of Schools
Berkshire Hills Regional School District
Stockbridge, MA

"In *The Wonder Wall* Peter Gamwell and Jane Daly speak with honesty, integrity, and insight about 'leading creative schools and organizations in an age of complexity' and express it all with wit, clarity, and humanity. A delight to read and a read that delights and informs—both clever and entertaining! This book is a must for anyone involved in leadership roles or with ambition to find a more successful model for management."

—Derek Brown, CEO
Actorshop
London, England

"*The Wonder Wall* has so many important and creative ideas, I suggest everyone read it more than once."

—Ellen J. Langer, Professor and Author
Harvard University
Cambridge, MA

To Pat
All best wishes
Peter

The Wonder Wall

To Liz,
You inspire me.
Peter

To John,
Thanks for everything.
Jane

The Wonder Wall

Leading Creative Schools and Organizations in an Age of Complexity

Peter Gamwell

Jane Daly

Foreword by Sir Ken Robinson

A Joint Publication

CORWIN
A SAGE Publishing Company

ONTARIO
PRINCIPALS'
COUNCIL
Exemplary Leadership in Public Education

FOR INFORMATION:

Corwin

A SAGE Company

2455 Teller Road

Thousand Oaks, California 91320

(800) 233-9936

www.corwin.com

SAGE Publications Ltd.

1 Oliver's Yard

55 City Road

London EC1Y 1SP

United Kingdom

SAGE Publications India Pvt. Ltd.

B 1/I 1 Mohan Cooperative Industrial Area

Mathura Road, New Delhi 110 044

India

SAGE Publications Asia-Pacific Pte. Ltd.

3 Church Street

#10-04 Samsung Hub

Singapore 049483

Executive Editor: Arnis Burvikovs

Senior Associate Editor: Desirée A. Bartlett

Editorial Assistant: Kaitlyn Irwin

Production Editor: Amy Schroller

Copy Editor: Mark Bast

Typesetter: C&M Digitals (P) Ltd.

Proofreader: Dennis W. Webb

Indexer: Sheila Bodell

Cover Designer: Scott Van Atta

Marketing Manager: Nicole Franks

Printed in the United States of America

Library of Congress Cataloging-in-Publication Data

Names: Gamwell, Peter, author. | Daly, Jane, author.

Title: The wonder wall: leading creative schools in an age of complexity / Peter Gamwell, Jane Daly.

Description: Thousand Oaks, California: Corwin, [2018] | Includes bibliographical references and index.

Identifiers: LCCN 2017001040 | ISBN 9781506357379 (pbk. : alk. paper)

Subjects: LCSH: Educational leadership. | Creative thinking. | Organizational change.

Classification: LCC LB2806 .G29 2018 | DDC 371.2—dc23 LC record available at https://lccn.loc.gov/2017001040

This book is printed on acid-free paper.

17 18 19 20 21 10 9 8 7 6 5 4 3 2 1

Contents

Foreword

It's common to say the world is changing faster than ever before. But it really is. The implications for how we organize our communities, businesses, and systems of education are immense. How do we run organizations that are stable enough to get the job done but flexible enough to adapt to the unpredictable changes that are happening all around them? That's what this book is all about, and Peter Gamwell is uniquely placed to write it.

After a lifetime in leadership positions in the complex world of public education, he knows only too well the awkward realities that face anyone who wants to bring about fundamental change in the way things are done in established systems and institutions. And that is the primary focus of the book. It's one thing, he says, to be creative in starting up new organizations: It's quite another to stimulate and lead innovation in places where taken-for-granted priorities and habits have long hardened into a fixed corporate culture. Then what do you do to effect change?

To answer that question, Gamwell draws on his own extensive experience of leading change in various systems of education, and he draws on multiple examples of leaders in other fields as diverse as sport, entertainment, technology, and auto-body work. Along the way he deftly captures the pragmatic ways in which creativity and innovation can be stimulated and harnessed by bringing the best out of people in every sort of organization: from families to project teams, from the classroom to the boardroom.

A common theme threading throughout the book is a deep conviction that everybody in every organization has often untapped creative capacities. The challenge for leaders is to cultivate flexible working relationships, rooted in collaboration and a shared vision, that develop these capacities in ways that benefit everyone in the organization and the vitality and success of the organization as a whole.

As they develop their argument, Peter and his coauthor, Jane Daly, distinguish what they describe as this "strength-based" approach with what they see as the deficits of the "problem-solving" model, which is more common in conventional approaches to organizational development and decision making. They relate these two approaches to Carol Dweck's conception of growth and fixed mind-sets and show how moving from one to the other can have a huge and positive impact, not only on individuals within the organization but on the energy, adaptability, and creativity of the entire organization.

I've known Peter Gamwell in various incarnations for almost 30 years. He approaches this book as he has all his work, throughout his professional life—with candor, passion, irrepressible wit, and a deep sense of humanity. Consequently, this book isn't just another bag of tricks for managing organizational change. It is a heartfelt, deeply grounded manifesto for the more visionary and creative styles of servant leadership we urgently need in every type of organization if we're to meet the unprecedented challenges we all face in common.

—Sir Ken Robinson
April 2017

Preface

There are a couple of things I'd like you to know about me. I've always found nature inspiring, and I have a deep suspicion of people with tidy desks. Having an office in my backyard solves both issues. I am surrounded by fresh air and nature (most significantly squirrels, chipmunks, and raccoons), and my mess is contained in my own small domain. I find I do my best thinking and socializing in that small, detached office, more conventionally known as my shed.

My shed has become something of a sanctuary for me. I do all kinds of work in there, brainstorming and writing and thinking. So it was only natural that when I began to frame out and capture the ideas contained here in *The Wonder Wall*, I took to my shed. Along with plenty of notepads and pens, oversized sheets of paper, and sticky notes.

It started out well. But I soon realized I was going to need a bigger shed. You see, this book has been a work in progress for 38 years. And it only really began to take shape around 2011, when I was trying to frame out a presentation I had been invited to give.

I had recently embarked on a reflection period in the shed, trying to figure out what had left me uninspired by my messaging in a previous presentation and what I could do to reshape and reposition my ideas.

How can we lead learning cultures that inspire and foster the unique and creative capacities that rest, too often dormant, in the individuals in our classrooms, business organizations, and even families? What are the characteristics of vibrant learning communities?

I decided that for my next presentation, I would do something a little different, something that more richly described my concepts and beliefs about learning, leadership, and creativity.

I had a solid research background, and my ideas had been shaped by some fresh and inspiring thinkers. Margaret Wheatley's principles of community that connect living systems theory with organizational health. Teresa Amabile's research in business organizations about the need to foster conditions that catalyze the potential and creative genius of each person. Ellen Langer's work that so eloquently describes the importance of imbuing our learning environments with uncertainty, rather than certainty. The idea that things in our world are shifting and changing with such exponential speed that as soon as you think you have a grasp on something, you probably don't know it at all, because it's changed.

My career in education had given me a foundation of rich experiences, as I had in my own way tried to create learning environments that were novel, inclusive, and ultimately that mattered to the individuals I was responsible for teaching or leading.

How could I weave my research foundation with my practical experience (that's the 38 years!) and, through sharing my story, help others interested in leading creative organizations in these complex times?

THE CHART, THE STICKIES, AND THE EMERGENCE OF STRUCTURE

I decided to figure it all out one weekend. First, I brought out the large fold-out chart and lots of sticky notes and Sharpie markers. Then, I spent an inordinate amount of time doing anything but the task at hand—a sort of extended gestation period. I've discovered this is a characteristic of my own learning process. To the untrained eye it might appear as though I'm not doing anything. This theory would be supported by my wife and children. However, after drinking untold cups of tea and coffee, checking the news, watching a couple of episodes of *Coronation Street*, one or two games of football (English football, specifically Everton), and a rugby game, I eventually took the top off of a Sharpie and wrote down four questions.

Why creativity and why now?

How can you make the extraordinary happen?

What are the conditions critical to fostering healthy and creative learning cultures?

Where do you start, and how do you assess your progress?

After this I was exhausted, so I went for a nap.

Upon awakening, I looked at the questions and realized that if I could develop these queries (which I actually thought were quite good!), I would have a reasonable presentation. I gathered more stickies and expanded my ideas around these guiding questions. And as so often happens, I ended up posing more questions, and more, until I found myself with a presentation.

Over the next several years, this structure grew and morphed as I presented to all manner of organizations, from Canada to Argentina and from

Oklahoma to Australia. From sectors in education, to municipal governments, to arts conferences and business seminars. It was a fascinating journey. And each time I presented, more ideas would emerge from not only myself, but from the audience, and my thinking would shift.

But only so much. The four core questions I wrote down that day, the ideas that to me are absolutely critical, remained. And that told me something: I was on the right track. The four questions formed the heart of what I was trying to communicate, and they resonated with people. They are timeless and relevant.

Those questions became the structure for this book. Sort of. When dealing with topics as complex as learning and creativity, you quickly find that nothing is linear. It's messy. It's why I chose sticky notes to organize my thoughts—because I can, and did, move them around. Endlessly. I still do. I often find ideas and exemplars that support one principle are also ideally suited to supporting others. I immersed myself in the world of uncertainty, while at the same time holding on to the structure of those four questions.

Eventually, I was encouraged to write these ideas into a book, by others who believe our educational structures and practices need to be challenged, reshaped, redesigned, and reimagined. This is not easy. Not everyone is comfortable with change. And that's why I want to tell this story—to inspire and reassure educators and other leaders that we will all benefit if our schools are structured in a way that allows for personalization and can unleash the potential in every student, teacher, staff member, and individual involved in the broader community. The same holds true when our businesses and organizations bring out the most creative ideas within their people.

THE WONDER WALL

What This Book Is About

Why Creativity? Why Now?

In the last few years, there has been an explosion of interest in creativity. From advertising to science, books and social media, sports, the arts, business, the trades; everywhere you look, people are talking about imagination, creativity, and innovation.

Why is this so? What is it about our current reality that gives rise to this interest?

This book explores this theme and draws on the ideas of the late Dr. Robert (Bobby) Moore, a remarkable visionary whose ideas help us to understand the role of human imagination and creativity, especially in times of significant societal shift.

How Can We Make the Extraordinary Happen?

My quest to seek possible new directions for our learning environments led me to some interesting places. Some of the most intriguing ideas and novel approaches lay outside education, in the business world. Most notably start-up companies who understand that to bring out the best in their people, they must embed cultures of learning that recognize creativity resides in everyone. And then foster conditions to make that happen.

Most of us don't work in start-ups. Most of us work in organizations that have been around for decades, whose organizational structures are founded in bureaucracies and practices that are entrenched. How can we make the extraordinary happen in these organizations?

To answer that question, this book describes the three imperatives we believe are critical for creativity to flourish. We also take you through a personal leadership initiative I was fortunate enough to lead with the Ottawa-Carleton District School Board, to shift the organizational learning culture and unleash the potential that lies within individuals, groups, and the organization itself. In many ways, it was inspired by Margaret Wheatley's (1992) living systems concept that the health of any system is intricately connected to and dependent on the delicate balance of its subsystems.

What Are the Conditions Necessary for Healthy and Creative Individuals and Organizations to Flourish?

If we want to make the extraordinary happen, to create learning cultures that foster and encourage the brilliance that lies within each person, then we need to figure out what conditions are necessary for that to happen. Think of your home, your family, your friends, your workplace. When people are really at their creative best, what's going on to help make that happen? What is the environment like? The range of responses I receive when I pose this question to audiences is remarkable. It's natural there will be different primary conditions depending on who and where you are.

Later in the book, we reveal the four conditions we believe are most effective to fostering creative learning. There are many more, of course, but drawing on my own research base and practical experience, these are, for me, the ones that have proven essential:

1. Storytelling and listening

2. Moving beyond diversity to inclusivity

3. Making it personal

4. Celebrating

Where Do You Start, and How Do You Assess Your Progress?

The first thing you need to do is gauge the temperature of your organization. How are people feeling? What are they telling each other that they're afraid to tell you? What's the truth of your culture? These questions are a great place to start, and there are other ideas and insights woven throughout *The Wonder Wall* for you to consider. The final chapter also provides a more fulsome set of suggestions to assess your culture of creativity.

WHAT YOU'LL FIND THROUGHOUT *THE WONDER WALL*

Stories. I'm a firm believer in the power of storytelling, and each chapter features stories and anecdotes to provide a glimpse into the worlds of people who, in their unique contexts, are fostering creativity in their own spheres of influence, making the world a far grander and more innovative place.

Implications for schools and school systems. We live in incredibly complex times and need to think about the role schools can play in shaping society and how our organizations can address these complexities. Each chapter regarding the four conditions also contains practical suggestions on how these ideas can be implemented within education systems, school districts, schools, and most importantly, classrooms.

Implications for the broader community. In our age of complexity, the success of students can't be left to an individual educator in a classroom. It does indeed take a village and the synergy of partnerships. We have to look to models and constructs across different sectors and learn from the best of what is being tried in business, government, communities, and every other corner of society. Great ideas exist everywhere. That is why *The Wonder Wall* explores not only the education sector but also searches outside our organizations for what works. After all, schools don't exist in a vacuum, and learning doesn't stop upon graduation.

Schools are a key component of the broader community. As living systems theory tells us, a healthy school helps foster a healthy community, as those students eventually leave the school to take on roles and display leadership in places of employment, families, neighborhoods, community teams and events, and more. Likewise, an unhealthy community will have an adverse effect on the school environment, as we see all too often in communities where students arrive at school hungry or dressed in inadequate clothing for the weather.

For this reason, *The Wonder Wall* doesn't separate education from its broader community, and we have included applicable anecdotes, examples, and insights from many sectors. The more success we have in creating a shared responsibility for education, the more likely we will be to reach and inspire all our students—and the more likely we will have planted the seeds for people to flourish in the broader community.

What This Book Isn't About

Although we provide lots of practical tips and guidelines in *The Wonder Wall*, we don't pretend to have all the answers or that we can hand you a one-size-fits-all solution to discover what conditions will foster creativity in your organization. Learning organizations are complex entities, no matter what form they take. A family, a board of directors, a classroom, or an NGO are all messy, turbulent, and intertwined entities. There is thus no one strategy, or a sequence of processes, that will result in the perfect organization. *The Wonder Wall* acknowledges the complexity of our times and provides some imperatives and conditions that you might consider as you make sense of your own journey. If you like, it provides a suggested structure around which to play with your own ideas. And when you discover your own ideas and ways to make the extraordinary happen, I hope you will share your insight with me.

—Peter Gamwell

Acknowledgments

The Wonder Wall has resulted from support, encouragement, and advice from many, many people over the course of countless years. Unfortunately, far too many to mention, both the people and, alas, the years. However, there are some people I must mention.

First I would like to thank my cowriter Jane Daly for her wisdom, brilliance, wit, and annoying persistence in challenging and pushing my ideas. She embarked on this journey with me at a time when we had no idea whether the book would be published. We just knew we had to write it.

A huge thanks to my literary manager (and literary lion) Peter Miller, who took a chance on me as a completely unknown entity and, after the first awkward phone call (who are you again?), gave me that breakthrough opportunity to write a proposal. His guidance and support made everything else possible. It was toward the end of March 2016 that Arnis Burvikovs from Corwin called to express interest in the book. He asked how long we would need to write it. I said about a year. He said August. I bought a defibrillator and started writing. Since that time, he and Desirée Bartlett have provided amazing support and advice as we honed the final version. Thank you.

Another huge thanks to Joanne Robinson, Ian McFarlane, and Ontario Principals' Council for their encouragement and support.

Although there are indeed way too many people to thank, I would like to acknowledge the following: Frank Wiley, Karyn Carty Ostafichuk, Jacqueline Lawrence, Lorri Huppert, Steve Massey, Susan McCalmont, George Tzougros, Tom Benke, and my many colleagues and friends at the Ottawa-Carleton District School Board. To Dr. Jennifer Adams, director of the Ottawa-Carleton District School Board, your support allowed the Lead the Way leadership initiatives to flourish for the past five years, and this is very much appreciated. My thanks to all of you for your ongoing interest and input. It has been so much appreciated and important in so many ways—if a little challenging at times!

Thanks to Andy Hargreaves, Sir John Jones, and Richard Gerver for such helpful feedback on the emerging text.

Huge appreciation to Jodi Rose. For your encouragement, advice, and incredible support. Thanks, Jodi.

Most importantly, by far, thank you to my family. My wife Liz, our children Adam and Laura, and their spouses Lisa and Dave. You are all amazing and so successful in helping me stay modest by reminding me of the mediocrity of many of my ideas. The endless and diverse topics of conversations, discussions, stories, disagreements, hilarity, occasional sulking, usually mixed with a spattering of love and mutual respect, are ever present at our gatherings. And have significantly shaped and exemplify the spirit and ideas of creativity and belonging that I hope are captured through these pages. Thank you all. You are inspiring.

A thanks to "Gran," my mum, for imbuing us with resilience and for encouraging us to embrace the world. She was a tour de force in a manner that was inimitable and lives on through her grandchildren.

And thank you to those whose stories and passions form the examples upon which the ideas of *The Wonder Wall* so heavily rely. Thank you so much for your generosity in sharing in such a personal and meaningful way. It's what puts the Wonder in *The Wonder Wall*.

I would be remiss if I didn't say a word about the person who has probably most helped shape my thinking and work in the area of creativity and learning. When I first heard Sir Ken Robinson speak many years ago, he did for me what I believe he has done for so many others. He provided a framework for the beliefs I had held for many years and a language that helped me understand more profoundly the importance of human creativity. And that it lies in everyone. He is a unique practical visionary.

I know I will have omitted some important names. My apologies. Please know that I appreciate you all.

PUBLISHER'S ACKNOWLEDGMENTS

Corwin gratefully acknowledges the contributions of the following reviewers:

Peter Dillon, Superintendent of Schools
Berkshire Hills Regional School District
Stockbridge, MA

Jill Gildea, Superintendent
Fremont School District
Mundelein, IL

Lynn Lisy-Macan, Visiting Assistant Professor
University at Albany–SUNY
Albany, NY

Jeff Ronneberg, Superintendent
Spring Lake Park Schools
Spring Lake Park, MN

Karen L Tichy, Assistant Professor of Educational Leadership
Saint Louis University, School of Education
St Louis, MO

About the Authors

 **Peter Gamwell** Born in Liverpool, Peter Gamwell is an author, presenter, and an award-winning leader in education who has worked in both central and eastern Canada and abroad. He is recently retired from the role of superintendent, responsible for district leadership development with the 75,000-student Ottawa-Carleton District School Board (OCDSB), where he also served as the board lead for Aboriginal education from 2006 until 2012.

Working closely with such renowned creativity experts as Sir Ken Robinson and Sir John Jones, Peter has become recognized nationally and internationally as a leader and catalyst for districtwide initiatives that inspire and advance education; student, faculty, community, and business engagement; and strength-based models and creative thinking. He has developed numerous presentations and papers on these topics and is regularly invited to speak both nationally and internationally.

With a reputation for engaging, compelling, and practical ideas, Peter has advised academia, the business community, and government departments at all levels on how to develop strategy to imbue creativity throughout an organization, as well as to create environments for optimal learning and engagement. Peter has been invited to sit on the Global Distinguished Leadership Panel at the Canadian Principals' Association conference, Banff, Alberta, and on the creativity expert panel at the World Creativity Forum in Oklahoma, and was appointed to the board of directors for the U.S.-based National Creativity Network.

In his spare time, Peter plays in a blues/rock band and has been featured as an entertainer on provincial and national radio and television. He lives in Ottawa, Canada, with his wife, Liz, and has two grown children.

Jane Daly Curious about the interconnections among creativity, education, and business, Jane Daly was happy to join Peter Gamwell in 2011 on his quest to discover more about the conditions that foster creativity. Jane works as a communications strategist and commercial writer by day and enjoys fiction writing by night, as well as spending time with her husband John, their kids and grandkids, and their dog and cat in Ottawa, Canada.

Prologue

The Wonder Wall

One of the great privileges of having served as a school superintendent was that I got to witness the miracle of learning right before my eyes. A short while before I retired, I visited a kindergarten classroom. Four children were seated at a mini conference table with their teacher. They were clearly engaged in some very heady work, poring over large sheets of paper.

"Well," I said. "What's going on here? This looks fascinating!"

One of the young lads looked up at me and said, "It *is* fascinating! Why don't you come and join us?"

I obliged and folded my tall body up like a paper clip into one of the tiny plastic chairs and asked Gloria, the teacher, what was going on.

"You see the chart over there?" she asked, pointing to a whiteboard hung at a child's height. "That's our Wonder Wall. Whenever the children become curious about something—or are wondering about something—they write it down on the Wonder Wall. Then we see if anyone else is interested in the topic and develop learning activities based around their interests."

I took a glance at the Wonder Wall and saw that it

included some very intriguing questions, such as, "How do my eyes stay in my head?"

"Anyway," Gloria continued, "one little boy was curious about how the human body works, and these other children decided they, too, would like to learn more about it. So you have now joined the Kindergarten Expert Panel on the Human Body."

Wow! I was honored to have joined such an auspicious group.

On the table in front of the children were large sheets of paper divided into three columns. The first column included pictures of different parts of the human body, the second column had the names associated with those body parts, and the third column was blank. The idea was for the children to share their knowledge about the various body parts and talk about where they were located, their function, what happened when they didn't function—and then document their learning.

"Right," I said. "Show me how this works!"

Gloria pointed to a picture of the intestines and asked one of the children if he could tell us what they were called.

He screwed up his face in anguish. He tapped a finger to his forehead and said, "I *used* to know this!"

Mind you, he was all of four years old.

But just then, he remembered.

"I know what it is!" he exclaimed.

Teacher Gloria puffed with pride. The brilliance of her teaching strategy was about to be demonstrated by her protégé right in front of the school superintendent.

"Tell us!" she encouraged.

"It's the intesticles!" the boy shouted. "The intesticles!"

It was certainly an answer I'll never forget.

That was my first experience with the Wonder Wall. What fascinated me most about it was that rather than the teacher guiding the students through a lesson, she had allowed them to take the lead, to follow their own natural curiosity, wherever it led them. The result was engagement, imagination, creativity, and learning.

I soon began thinking about how the concept of the Wonder Wall could have intriguing possibilities for learning in situations way beyond kindergarten. And as I began looking around at school boards, businesses, organizations, government, and our communities, I found I was right.

I believe the Wonder Wall is a metaphor that can help spur on our learning environments and our society to transformational change. That's why it inspired the title of this book: *The Wonder Wall: Leading Creative Schools and Organizations in an Age of Complexity.*

Just before we begin, I would like to point out that whereas this book refers frequently to our educational systems, the ideas and practical suggestions can be applied to anyone or any group striving to become more successful and innovative. Whether you are a classroom or a school board, a family, a sports team, a charity or group of volunteers, a business, a community, or simply an individual looking to become more creative, I believe you will find the same value and inspiration of that young kindergarten class in *The Wonder Wall*.

Sincerely,
Peter Gamwell

The Start of Something Extraordinary

"If I must start somewhere, right here and right now is the best place imaginable."

—Richelle E. Goodrich

Many of us experience a pivotal conversation early in our lives when someone important, often an adult who knows us well, encourages us to do something that will make the world a better place. One of my pivotal moments began like this:

"Gamwell, why don't you just go get a job?"

These words were uttered by a teacher in Liverpool, England, as I was lining up to enroll for my next level of courses. To my impressionable 16-year-old self, the statement not only boiled down into one sentence my entire 11 years of school achievement but also pronounced the grim level of potential the teacher saw in me. In his opinion, continuing on with higher education would be a waste of my time—as well as everybody else's.

More than four decades have passed since that meeting, and the man who declared my poor prognosis is, by now, certainly retired. (I believe his heart had already retired at the time of our meeting.)

Lest you feel sorry for that poor young lad that was I in Liverpool, let me be quick to point out this is a good-news story. In hindsight, that short inter-action with the teacher and his one-sentence synopsis of my future was something of a catalyzing moment. I have often recalled his words during my teaching career, and they have influenced the way I look at the potential of students, particularly those who have struggled academically, like me.

The truth is, I graduated from high school having very little idea of what I would be good at.

WHY WAS THAT?

I started thinking about it. It wasn't as if many of my teachers hadn't done a remarkable job of documenting the things I was bad at. I have to admit my behavior was not always the best. And so they had dutifully taken the time to point this out to me, both spontaneously in the classroom and at regularly mandated meetings throughout my school career! The list included not only academic shortcomings but also my penchant for disrupting the class.

I want to make it clear that I don't blame the teachers. They were simply following what were considered standard practices. Rather than look at my young self and wonder what untapped potential I might hold, my teachers believed the secret to my success was to correct all the things that were *wrong* with me. If I was bad at math exercises, then I must be given more math exercises. If I hated reading, then more reading I must do. If I couldn't sit still in class, then I must get detention and spend even more time sitting still after class (or, at least, trying to).

And so, as my school career drew to a close, whatever things I was capable of, whatever things sparked a light in me, if there was anything at all I truly excelled at—that knowledge had, for the most part, eluded my teachers and me. I didn't realize that perhaps I was someone who, despite his distractibility, might have a keen insight in how to teach, strategically plan, create music. Not because I didn't have capabilities but because the capabilities I possessed didn't fall within the narrowly defined parameters of what learning, success, and potential looked like. Having failed to measure up to what was then defined as a promising student, I was deemed to have little promise at all.

EXCEPT, PERHAPS, FOR GETTING A JOB SOMEWHERE

I said this was a good-news story, and rest assured that it is. My brief encounter with my teacher that day provided me with a profound insight, one that comprises a most important imperative I believe is essential for creating environments that foster creativity and innovation. That first imperative is the belief that every person, regardless of rank, background, social status, or school grades, possesses a seed of brilliance. It's taken me some four decades, a career in education spanning from England to Canada, and help from a team of thousands to figure out two more imperatives and four primary conditions that foster creative environments, but that moment with my teacher is where it all began. It was the first step on my journey to something extraordinary.

Over the years, as I began to formulate my thoughts, I found the topic of creativity resonated with many other people, and we were all eager to connect and exchange ideas. I was extremely fortunate to learn from some very great minds on the topic, such as Ellen Langer, Sir Ken Robinson,

Daniel Pink, Margaret Wheatley, Teresa Amabile, Sir John Jones, and many others who have devoted their careers to creativity and innovation. I also had the pleasure of working with the Lead the Way to Creativity campaign with the Ottawa-Carleton District School Board (OCDSB) in Canada's national capital, which included thousands of participants who shared their ideas.

Interestingly, those who contacted me or engaged me to speak publicly to their groups came not just from the field of education but from other industry sectors such as government, medicine, creative think tanks, businesses, not-for-profits, engineering groups, and even utility companies. Moreover, some of the most invigorating conversations I've had on the subject took place in coffee shops, airport lounges, and the checkout at the grocery store.

I believe part of this interest has been sparked because so many organizations today are wondering how to become more innovative in general, especially in an increasingly global society. And, as it turns out, the hierarchies, processes, and philosophies involved in running school boards and making our classrooms and student learning environments flourish are not that much different from those of the organizations we build for us grown-ups—thus the same imperatives and conditions that foster creative environments in schools can easily be applied to any organization or undertaking.

This is especially true when you consider that all organizations are involved in learning: learning how to succeed, learning about what their clients want, learning what products or services will work for them, learning about the risks and opportunities out there, learning how they can make the world a better place. We're not so removed from our school days after all, especially when our changing world requires us to constantly update our knowledge and skills to stay competitive. Schools and various organizations also share a vested interest in creativity, because the more creative our students are in the classroom, the more creative they will be in the boardroom.

For several years, schools have focused on a back-to-basics movement (as have many businesses and organizations). Along with standardized curriculum and standardized testing (cousins of lean processing, setting objectives, and annual reviews in the business world), educators are strongly encouraged to recognize and reward competence in two main areas—math and language. We need standards and levels of achievement in math and language because they support learning of so many other subjects. Common sense tells us that once a student masters reading, for example, it provides the key to read and learn more about virtually any subject in the world.

But taken too far, the problem with narrow and rigid standardization is that children—and adults—are not standardized, as Sir Ken Robinson (2011) has often pointed out. And moreover, standardization is the very antithesis of innovation. If we are really serious about setting up environments in schools and organizations that foster creativity and innovation, then we must do the hard work of figuring out how we make the extraordinary happen.

In my own quest to figure this out, during my dewy-eyed early days of teaching, I wanted to help my students to find their passion, to learn "what they were good at"—so that they didn't end up like me, not knowing this basic information about themselves on the last day of high school.

At first glance, the answer seems obvious: A student is good at whatever subject he or she scores high marks in. But I soon learned that wasn't the whole story. Not nearly so. I realized that a student who scored perfectly on a spelling test didn't necessarily have a deeper understanding of literacy or even an interest in the subject, let alone a passion; it often meant he had good memorization skills. It was the same for learning multiplication tables or a musical score. Learning something, being competent at it or even mastering it, could still result in glazed-eyed boredom. It did not magically lead to engagement or passion or mean the student would want to take up a career doing it.

CLEARLY I WAS MISSING SOMETHING, BUT WHAT?

Then one day I was feeling a bit rebellious and decided to change things up a bit. Joining forces with a few other teachers, we asked permission for the school to put on a rock opera, *Jesus Christ Superstar*. Mind you, the title choice was somewhat unconventional and risky, especially because this was a Catholic high school in a rather polite community. Happily, they allowed us to do it anyway.

The production of *Jesus Christ Superstar* completely transformed the way I look at learning and education. There was no curriculum set out; we were all just flying by the seat of our pants. We had only one rule: Anyone who wanted to be a part of the musical was a part of the musical. We had auditions only for the lead roles, and everyone else just gravitated toward whatever sparked their interest, from set design to costumes to special effects—whether they had any prior experience or learning in the subject mattered not.

It might sound like a script for disaster, but in the end, the only word that could adequately sum up the project is *magical*. Members of the audience, the cast, and the crew left the performances exclaiming, "That was amazing!" Not "That was amazing—for a high school performance," but "That was amazing." Period. Lest you think I'm exaggerating, I recently found out there is an active Facebook group that was formed by students to reminisce about their experiences in putting on that rock opera, even though it all happened some 40 years ago!

What was most magical, however, even gobsmacking, was the incredible amount of learning that took place across all subjects, from acting and math to engineering and science to design and art. And by learning, I mean *learning* and engagement, not simply memorization. Especially given our lack of experience, we ran into challenges, lots of them, but each time, everyone worked together, contributing their knowledge and ideas, to figure out a way around it. We invited the broader community in, forming partnerships and tapping into their expertise. We even had the military come in, to teach us about precision in movements. The students benefitted enormously from this community knowledge, and I believe the community benefitted as well.

And there was passion—parents often complain they have a hard time getting their kids to come to school, but we couldn't get them to go home! Everyone wanted to stay well after the bell rang and keep working on the musical.

Of course I was delighted with the outcome of the rock opera project, but I was curious: What was it that sparked such enthusiasm and engaged learning among the students? (And for that matter, the teachers and the community as well?) How had we managed to bring out that spark of brilliance in each student involved? And most importantly, how could I replicate this phenomenon in the classroom?

I understood at least part of the appeal of the project was that it was different, it was fun, and it was novel. But it seemed to me there was something more. How was using math to design a stage set really all that different from using math to solve a problem in the classroom?

Looking back, after years went by and I learned more on my quest, it eventually came to me. It wasn't that we were teaching the students through the rock opera project and helping them learn what they were good at. It was the other way around: The rock opera set the conditions for the students' brilliance and unique abilities, what was already inside them, to emerge. And they discovered themselves what sparked their curiosity and passion, took ownership for their learning, and discovered what they were good at.

SIGNIFICANTLY, THIS WAS THE ENVIRONMENT NEEDED FOR CREATIVITY TO FLOURISH

Let me explain further. A common belief is that learning has taken place when the student can demonstrate what he or she has been taught: the ability to solve a math equation, write an essay in a desired format, or read sheet music to play a song on the piano.

Creativity, however, is the ability to go *beyond* any skills or knowledge that has been taught: to come up with a new mathematical theory; to persuade others to a course of action through written words; to compose music.

Conventional wisdom holds that before you can be creative in a certain area, you must first have mastered the learning. How can you write a song before you have learned to read notes? But the more I learn about creativity, the more I realize this is seldom the case. More often, it's creativity—the wonder walls, the innovation, and the "what if's"—that sparks and drives the learning.

Following this realization, I read dozens, if not hundreds, of books and articles as I sought to learn more about creativity and how to teach and impart its gifts to my students. Most of these books set out a formula to teach people or groups how to become creative. There were exercises to free the mind, individual and group brainstorming tips, self-hypnosis, yoga, and meditation techniques.

I've no doubt these methods work for some people, and that was my problem with them. There's no one-size-fits-all way to teach creativity, and in a classroom of 30 pupils (or a department of 30 employees or more!) how does a teacher or team leader have the time to find and teach different methods to each student? Even if we could find a method that suited each student and convince them to apply it, isn't creativity using the same standardized process a bit of a logical oxymoron?

Likewise, whereas I'm sure these methods could be very effective for some, the results simply couldn't compare to the extraordinary ones we had accomplished through *Jesus Christ Superstar*—a project in which, ironically, we hadn't even been trying to teach creativity.

THE ANSWERS CONTINUED TO ELUDE ME

Then one day, I was jamming with some friends, playing my piano and having a great time of it. We were fairly good musicians, having practiced our skills and playing regularly through the course of our lives. We were all playing together, but each of us was doing our own creative thing as well, building on what the others were doing and making the music even better than what would have been set out on music sheets.

As any musician can tell you, it's a wonderful place to be, playing in a band. That day, everyone was included, we all took turns soloing, and everyone brought something different to the table. We weren't afraid to take a risk musically; we knew we would learn from trying out new things and none of us would judge. Our primary goal was to make the music the best it could be, each of us complementing the other. The mood was celebratory, and everyone was feeling grand. Yet no one had come in and taught or instructed our band members to do these creative things; we simply let loose in that trusting environment, and learning followed naturally.

That's when it began to dawn on me. It wasn't that someone had *taught* us to be creative or to master music; it was the *environment* that allowed and encouraged our seeds of brilliance and leadership abilities, which we already possessed, to come forth.

I realized that a similar cultural environment had been created during the rock opera. Everyone was included. Everyone was recognized as having diverse creative and leadership abilities, many as yet unknown, which were needed to make the musical the best damn musical it could be. Students were given autonomy to follow their interests and tackle challenges that stretched their imaginations and learning in new and creative ways. The atmosphere was fun and celebratory. Everyone was learning new things. And the students were so engaged, they couldn't get enough of it.

Now the course of my research in creativity transformed to focus on the question "What are the conditions necessary to create environments that foster creativity?" This inspiring stage of my journey has connected me to thousands of people, from all backgrounds and all walks of life, who are equally interested in finding the answers.

For that reason, I've been encouraged for some time by various people to write down in a book what I've learned about innovation and leadership and particularly how certain conditions in an environment can organically foster creativity. I thought I might do so one day—once I had all of it figured out. I now realize that day will never come. I'm still continuing to learn. And I realize the nuances and applications of creativity are so immense, and the world is changing so rapidly, that no one would be able to lay out everything one needs to do to make a school district or organization creative in five easy steps.

Instead, what *The Wonder Wall* does is outline three imperatives and four primary conditions (there are dozens of subconditions) that I believe are most effective to setting up classrooms and work environments, processes and attitudes that work to foster innovation, creativity, and leadership.

If we can embed the imperatives and conditions necessary, these environments naturally bring out that seed of brilliance in each person, and the learning will follow organically under the student's eager lead. We can help a student learn dates of important events in history, but we must also create environments that bring out a student's creative ability to grasp insight between the past and the present and come up with solutions for the future if we want to make our schools, and the world, a better place.

I didn't heed the advice of the teacher that day who advised me not to pursue higher learning. I went on to get a degree in music and education, then spent 20 years teaching on Canada's rocky coast of Newfoundland and Labrador before moving to Ottawa and eventually becoming a school district superintendent with a focus on developing leadership and creativity.

I have become quite passionate about trying to figure out how we can balance the need for students to master the basics while also fostering environments where creativity flourishes.

This continues to be a provocative journey where I've often had to buck convention, but the response I've had from thousands of people confirm I'm not alone in my beliefs. I have been able to interview and connect with many remarkable people who have made great strides through our shared belief that we need to transform our educational and business environments if we are to be creative and successful and if we want to do the extraordinary. I have included some of these interviews here.

YOU MIGHT WANT TO READ THIS BOOK TWICE

I know this is an odd request, but I hope you will do me the favor of reading this book twice. The reason is that the three imperatives and four primary conditions that foster creativity don't line up all nice and neat on a linear path; they build upon each other, and there is a lot of overlap between them. The conditions support more than one imperative. A first read-through will give you a good understanding of these, but I feel a second read will truly help you understand the finer synergies and connections between them.

I've always invited others to share their insights into creativity, their ideas and experiences, and would be delighted if, after finishing this book—whether once or twice—you shared your thoughts with me by visiting my website, petergamwell.com, or e-mailing me at thewonderwall@petergamwell.com. Thank you for joining me on a journey to something extraordinary.

Conditions That Foster Creativity

The **three imperatives**:

1. Recognize there is a seed of brilliance in everyone.

2. Adopt a strength-based approach.

3. Create cultures of belonging.

The **four conditions**:

1. Storytelling and listening

2. Moving beyond diversity to inclusivity

3. Making it personal

4. Celebrating

2 A Funny Thing Happened on the Way to the Future

The Connection Between Change and Creativity

"When you can't change the direction of the wind, adjust your sails."

—H. Jackson Brown Jr.

Whenever I've felt confident about my ability to plan the course of my life, a funny thing happens on the way to the future. It's called *change*. You may have noticed the same thing.

The problem with change is we tend to build our future focused squarely on the past. Not just our personal past but on the entire history of humankind. We base our decisions on the things we have learned in the past, our past experiences, our past personal preferences—these all play key roles in shaping our future.

Likewise, our society forecasts the behavior of the economy based on past cycles. We decide when to plant and harvest based on past growing patterns of crops and consumer demand; we design educational curriculum to develop the skills and knowledge that have been valued and proven useful in the past.

Much of the time, this strategy works. But then the economy changes, making us rethink our plans for retirement; new inventions make jobs obsolete and bring untried opportunities; and quite distressing in my personal experience, the local pub no longer serves my favorite bacon butty.

Change not only upsets the carefully constructed apple carts, it also forces us to make decisions when we already had our hearts set on something else—and perhaps don't feel adequately equipped to make new plans. Will ordering the steak and kidney pie really satisfy my hunger, when I'm still missing my bacon butty?

For these reasons, it's not surprising that when we sense impending change in the air, many of us feel a distinct sense of unease.

Some of us, however, are better at embracing change than others. Perched on their rocky province on the east coast of Canada, Newfoundlanders and Labradoreans are a uniquely creative and interesting people, as anyone who has had the pleasure of visiting them will know. Their culture is innovative to its very core and exemplifies many of the themes explored in this book. Humorous, playful, politically astute, and masters of their own domain, their survival in a harsh climate is a testament to their individual and collective imagination.

It was in Newfoundland that I first met the late Dr. Robert (Bobby) Moore. Bobby held a broad variety of positions during his career, including as a teacher, a university lecturer, a radio broadcaster, and a theologian, all before being appointed as high commissioner to Canada for Guyana. When I was teaching in Newfoundland, we used to bring Bobby in quite often to talk to us about a variety of subjects and to provoke our thinking and our actions, things he was very good at.

TIMES OF INBETWEENITY: TIMES BETWEEN TIMES

It was on one such occasion that Bobby discussed why creativity, in his opinion, was the best pathway forward for our society. Bobby explained that we are living in a world of *inbetweenity*—a time in between times, when one era is on its way out, and the next era has not yet fully emerged. That bubble in between the two eras is a time of inbetweenity.

Bobby believed that during times of inbetweenity, the status quo no longer works, but at the same time, no one is quite sure what's going to happen next. For many people, inbetweenity is therefore a period of insecurities and unknowns; a time when individuals, organizations, and societies jockey for advantage in the face of changes that have not yet fully revealed themselves.

For me, the concept of inbetweenity provides an excellent perspective from which to view the "ages" the human race has braved in the past. These eras and ages are often heralded by significant social upheaval, such as war, pandemic, political uprising, economic boom or bust, or by a game-changing innovation such as the steam engine, printing press, internal combustion engine, airplane, medical advances, or the Internet. As such, each era appears, in retrospect at least, to have a fairly abrupt and identifiable beginning, and often a fairly distinct ending, brought about when the "Next Big Thing" came along.

In times past, society's ages and stages proceeded along at a much more leisurely pace. As far as day-to-day living was concerned, a person who fell asleep during the year 917 and woke up in the year 1017 would hardly notice the difference.

On the other hand, someone taking a century-long nap from 1917 to 2017 might well think they'd been shipped off to another planet. In fact, I've read that some experts believe the shock of experiencing such a change would be so unnerving that a real Rip Van Winkle might actually die, and I believe it. Every morning when I wake up and see how much the price of gas has changed overnight, I almost die myself.

TIMES OF INBETWEENITY HAVE EVOLVED TO TIMES OF COMPLEXITY

The upshot of this rapid rate of change is that eras are no longer politely waiting for a former age to leave the stage before emerging from the wings. Instead, we are seeing hundreds of ages and eras take the stage simultaneously across all spheres of society: educational, political, spiritual, economic, social, technological, medical, scientific, environmental, and many others. As a result, we have moved beyond the times when there could be a breath of inbetweenity between each new age as they moved along in a linear fashion. Instead, I believe we are now living in what could best be described as a *state of complexity*: a time when there are no longer beginnings or endings but rather a continuous confluence of changes.

This state of complexity impacts our world in three unprecedented ways.

1. **Changes push and pull us in all directions at once.** In times past, the world's ages were perceived as evolutionary stages of progress; generally, each stage built upon the lessons and developments of the previous one to sedately advance quality of life, knowledge, and reason. In states of complexity, however, we are evolving, devolving, revolving, and moving sideways, all at the same time. In fact, advances that are perceived to push one sphere of society forward, such as resource extraction, may be perceived to have a direct and negative impact on another, such as the environment.

2. **There is less consensus on what "progress" looks like or in which direction we should be trying to pull together.** With social media, we have all become news reporters as well as news consumers. Social media is also giving today's activists and lobbyists the ability to instantly communicate, recruit, and organize for their causes, facing off multiple stakeholder groups with opposing viewpoints to create a cacophony of confluence. Yet despite having easier, faster, and more prevalent means to communicate with each other today, we often react by trying to drown others out or prevent them from speaking. At the same time, the Internet enables myths, urban legends, false statistics, and even "fake" news stories to take on lives of their own.

3. **This complexity makes future trends more difficult—if not impossible—to predict.** Within the mathematical concept of chaos theory, complex systems are highly sensitive to changes in conditions, so even small alterations can result in disproportionate consequences—hypothetically, one small flap of a butterfly's wing can wreak catastrophic weather changes on the other side of the world. The puzzle of our global economic recovery demonstrates this. Whereas some top economists have been drawing on historic patterns to forecast an end to the global recession since 2010, today's global economy continues to baffle us, moving two steps forward, one step back, and three steps sideways—until we all might wonder if it will do the hokey-pokey next!

With this third impact, it's important to keep in mind that whereas modest changes to conditions in a complex system can lead to disproportionate results, those results aren't always negative. Take a look at the recent evolution of social media in which a single plea for help can be shared millions of times within a single day, helping to catch criminals and kidnappers; track down lost children, pets, friends, and family members; return lost teddy bears; and find funding not just for charitable causes but innovations, businesses, and personal dreams. In our new age of complexity, even a single person, such as yourself, making a single positive change can have a domino effect more quickly than ever before.

WHAT DOES THIS STATE OF COMPLEXITY HAVE TO DO WITH CREATIVITY?

Let's go back to Bobby Moore for a moment. In times of inbetweenity, when one age is on its way out and another is on its way in, people are often forced to get creative if they are going to survive. When an ice age is on the horizon, figuring out new ways to build sturdier shelters, stay warm, and secure new food sources is imperative; when a new technology makes your job obsolete, you must come up with ways to evolve your abilities and learn new skills. This is why times of change often go hand in hand with innovation.

For Bobby, there were three main ways in which people dealt with times of inbetweenity, or that space of time between major societal changes.

In the first group are those who attempt to stay rooted in the past, holding on to the status quo for dear life. They keep doing the same things, communicating the same information, engaging people in the same way, offering the same programs, and seeking funding from the same sources, as they have always done. For this group, change becomes a source of great anxiety, because no matter how hard they try to stop it, it's like trying to solve tomorrow's problems with yesterday's rules, or abolishing the future in the name of the past. It just doesn't work.

The second group, a rather analytical bunch, takes a line from the past and attempts to follow it into the future. They declare they want to accept change, but they try to deal with the uncertainty by projecting current or past trends within known, narrowly defined parameters. They will take what they already have and already know, perhaps announce a new transformational regime across their school board or organization, and hope it will work to address the evolving landscape of the sector. It's like writing new chapters onto a text that has already been written. That might work in a world where everything is expected to stay the same or change in slow and orderly incremental steps. But when major changes are afoot, what's often needed to survive and flourish is not adding new chapters onto an old text but writing a whole new book.

A third group, by contrast, embraces the developing uncertainties, employing a faculty of vision. These individuals understand that the way to lead others along a path of vision is to foster environments that harness imagination and creativity in pursuit of innovation. They use their imagination and their will not to control the future, nor to attempt to predict the future, but to *invent* it. They take not one line but many lines into the future, some old and some new, and weave them into patterns to form a new future—something that has never been seen before. These practical visionaries have the ability to construct in their imagination worlds that are not yet but can be.

I believe that in states of complexity, such as the one we are now experiencing, different groups of people react much the same as Bobby proposed in his times of inbetweenity, with one important difference: *the urge to control.*

The confluence of so many changes and variables makes it hard for people to even know where to begin sorting it all out, so they try to control the complexity, nail it down, put it into a plan, and contrive ways to monitor it, manage it, measure it, and mitigate it.

There are drawbacks to this approach. First, whereas no one is going to argue that research or planning are bad things, trying to pin down precisely what is happening during states of complexity can soon suck financial and human resources down into an infinite black hole. Things are changing so quickly and in so many different directions that by the time research or a study is complete, some of the variables may have changed considerably. Ironically, in a time when we can access the world's knowledge in an instant on the Internet, for every research paper that says one thing, you can find another that says the opposite. Attempting to endlessly find the One Right Answer or the One Perfect Solution may therefore be futile; it may be more advantageous to research a variety of flexible and nimble solutions, backup resources, and contingency plans.

In our classrooms, we need to teach students to answer the questions, but we also need to teach them to question the answers.

Another challenge with this approach is that we tend to become more rigid and inflexible as we try to control and subdue the complexity. Knowing there are numerous factors beyond our control, we may attempt to micro-manage those things that are within our grasp. Again, no one is going to argue that trying to control and mitigate those risks we are capable of predicting is a bad thing to do. But as with trying to master and forecast what's happening in a world of complexity, trying to focus too much on controlling things, including micromanaging the people and processes around you, can work against you and usually strangles innovation and ideas.

It's easy to see how this need to control becomes an attractive option in our educational and work environments. It often starts out when a company is faced with an actual or predicted weaker bottom line. To deal with this, top executives create mission and vision statements that are cascaded down the ranks to define, corral, and control all activities. Each team leader and employee is tasked with annual objectives and daily tasks to fulfill the mission and vision, and their progress will be rewarded or penalized accordingly. Organizational charts, process maps, and standardization flow charts are drawn up, letting people know which little box they fit into, what tasks they need to complete each day, and where their tasks fit within the big-picture process. If anyone has a question, one need only point to the established org chart, process chart, or decision-making chart to find the answer. The concept of stopping wastes—of time, money, and resources—becomes paramount.

It all sounds efficient and good in theory, and it certainly has its benefits. But in states of complexity, the urge to micro-control everything makes it easy for organizations to mistake lean processing, scheduling, measuring, and managing as the primary goal of their business or organization—when it should be how to make the world a better place. If they can put creativity and innovation to work to create a product or a service that can do that, monetary profits or other desired rewards and benefits should soon follow.

This concept of "lean processing" in business, nonprofits, and government is not too far removed from common approaches to educational processes. As budgets shrink and many postsecondary facilities find themselves competing on global and digital scales for a shrinking student population, there's an increasing incentive to standardize, scale efficiencies, do more with less, and monitor success through purely objective measures. This puts pressure on educational policymakers and teachers to "lean process" education, with one standard curriculum, approved processes to deliver the material, standardized tests to measure progress, and the like. Virtually every teacher I've spoken to would love to spend more time personalizing learning to best suit each individual student, but time constraints make this difficult.

TAKEN TOO FAR, LEAN PROCESSING IS LEAN ON INNOVATION

Schools, companies, organizations, and governments can focus so intently on this "lean processing" that they lose sight of the big picture. The process and the org chart become so rigidly entrenched that no one is allowed to step outside the lines. Team leaders are encouraged to ensure the same process is performed, with the same result, every time. This may work well for a time or in some areas, such as manufacturing, leading company executives to believe that rigid control is working for them. In fact, an initial success often reinforces the rationale to repeat the exact same process in an attempt to replicate the success and discourages innovation or new ways of doing things.

But as times change (and complexity reigns supreme), the end result of the process eventually becomes obsolete—and with no planned innovation in the company, the bottom line once again starts to suffer. Which, ironically, often encourages the top brass to step up the lean processing all the more!

Edward Hess (2015), professor of business administration at the Darden School of Business, University of Virginia, and author of 11 books, wrote about the need to balance lean processing with the need to innovate in his article, "Is Your Six Sigma Stifling Innovation?" You can see how closely related innovation is to learning:

Very soon, the tasks that Lean and Six Sigma have helped operationalize will be handled primarily by robots and smart machines. And that's a good thing. Nothing beats a robot in terms of efficiency and perfection. But here's the *real* question: How good is your company at doing all the things robots *can't* do well—such as innovate? . . . the *only* real competitive advantage these days is the ability to learn and innovate. That means your organization must be okay with risk—and the screw-ups, missteps, and waste that inevitably accompany it. The problem, of course, is that an organization steeped in the lore of Lean and Six Sigma naturally views them as sins to stamp out.

CREATIVITY HAS ALWAYS BEEN IMPORTANT, BUT IT'S EVEN MORE SO NOW

I believe creativity is increasingly important today because we are currently in a state of complexity. As discussed, the world has changed more in the last century than in the two millennia that went before it. We will never go back to times of inbetweenity, when ages and stages proceeded along in a polite, orderly fashion. States of complexity are here to stay.

For many people, not knowing what's going to happen next can be unsettling. In the past, when humans found themselves in a tough spot, it was often our ability to see correlations, make connections, and predict events that helped pull us through.

It's easy to see why we evolved this way. Certainly humans had a better chance of survival if they could predict when the herds would migrate and the blueberries would ripen, when the snow would arrive, and what time the local saber-toothed tiger liked to eat lunch. Today's Day-Timers and planners have stepped out of that primordial soup of correlation and cause and effect so we can plan and predict every aspect of our lives down into 15-minute time slots. Longer term, albeit less predictably, we forecast what the weather will be like for our Saturday garden party and surmise what skills students need to learn today to be productive, happy, and healthy members of society 20 years from now.

At the same time, despite our natural yearning for predictability, creativity is not a new concept. Greek, Roman, Persian, Indian, and Chinese civilizations had modern-type plumbing dating back nearly 5,000 years ago, and around the same time, the Finns invented ice skates from using sharpened animal bones. The Indus Valley Civilization was creating standardized measuring devices for length, weight, and time and practicing dentistry. There are countless examples of innovation that were created even before the first wheel was invented, let alone the other three—and today's scientists are still trying to figure out how some civilizations managed their feats of knowledge, skill, and engineering.

There is little doubt that a lot of humankind's innovative leaps came during times of inbetweenity and within our current state of complexity.

We could not have survived by using our instinct for predictability alone. But what I find most interesting is that innovation isn't always borne from the mother of necessity. Sometimes, innovation comes not from attempting to solve a problem or escape from impending doom but from aspiring to imagine "what could be"—an instinct to push forward the greater well-being of humankind.

CHANGING OUR FUTURES WITH A MIND-SET SHIFT

Carol Dweck, a researcher from Stanford University, is best known for her research into human motivation. In her theory she calls "mindset," the beliefs we develop about our own ability to learn can have a formative and powerful influence over who we become. She developed this theory while working with children, when she noticed two different mind-sets among them. Those with *fixed* mind-sets believed their abilities were predetermined, that they had a set intelligence and character with limited potential for change. On the other hand, those with *growth* mind-sets placed no such limitation on themselves. They felt their inborn assets were only a starting point—a belief that through effort, play, learning, and embracing possibility, they could change and grow continually.

I once heard another speaker say there are two types of people in the world: those who say there are two types of people in the world and those who don't. I should caution you that I fall into the latter category. Having only two types of people could get rather dull.

But what I find fascinating about Dweck's work is that the fixed mind-set group actually has the *same* potential for growth as the growth mind-set group; as far as potential goes, the two groups are, in fact, one and the same. Dweck (2006) sums this up succinctly when she says, "Mindsets are just beliefs. They're powerful beliefs, but they're just something in your mind, and you can change your mind" (p. 16).

The understanding and reality of Dweck's fixed and growth mind-sets has a profound impact on how individuals think and behave. I believe it also has huge implications for group and organizational learning.

Dweck is not the only one with this belief. Ellen Langer (1997), in her theory of "mindfulness," says we are taught to search for certainty. But once we are certain of something, we actually become *mindless*, no longer examining or analyzing the concept we think we know. Yet ironically, the thing we thought certain is no longer true, because everything is constantly changing. *Mindfulness* is the understanding that things look one way from one perspective but completely different from another. Learning happens when you notice new things. I believe this process of mindfulness is common to great thinkers across disciplines. They constantly vary the way in which they attend to things, allowing them to escape the bounds of convention, to free their imaginations to create new possibilities. This is what catalyzes human development.

Stories From the Field

The Fallacy of the Right Answer

Another interesting facet of how we humans approach our changing landscape is our urge to find an answer, usually to a problem. This is especially true in education. The then-director and CEO of the Canada Council of the Arts, Robert Sirman, who spoke to the Ottawa-Carleton District School Board Leadership Conference in 2009, describes this as "the fallacy of the right answer." Here's a paraphrased version of the story he told us that day, about growing up as a baby boomer in Toronto, Ontario's, public education system:

> The ease with which I advanced though this system resulted in my ending up with the misguided notion that getting ahead was based on being smart. For 18 years, I had been part of a system in which the rules remained relatively stable: Someone in authority would ask me a question, and if I gave the right answer, I could move forward. After many years of positive reinforcement, I believed that having the right answers was what was necessary to succeed in life. . . .

> Today I'd like to talk a bit about the fallacy of this logic. . . . The notion of the right answer I learned as a student is relatively simplistic, (like) someone answering a multiple-choice question. In our professional lives, especially in jobs that involve working with other people, it is rare to encounter challenges that are so one-dimensional in nature. Simplistic is the last word I would use to describe leading creative organizations.

> Leading creative organizations means making room for other people's input. It means having as a starting point a willingness to accept many different points of view and a recognition that everyone in the organization, no matter where they find themselves in the institutional hierarchy, has something of value to offer.

If what you are trying to achieve in leading creative organizations is positive outcomes, such outcomes have the highest probability of success when you can engage the creative contributions of as many people in your organization as possible. Compliance in creative organizations does not come from telling other people what to do, no matter how smart you might think you are, or how good your proposal, but by engaging them in determining a shared course of action.

WHAT PEOPLE CAN LEARN FROM PALM TREES

When organizations refuse to bend during a state of complexity, they ultimately tend to break. Nature has evolved that way. Picture how a palm tree bends and sways in the face of a hurricane, when winds are pulling it in all directions, and you'll understand why flexibility is essential during a state of complexity. Unfortunately, organizations too often take the opposite approach. The more chaotic and confusing the world becomes, the harder they hold on to "the way things have always been done" and resist implementing the conditions that would help creativity, innovation, and success to flourish. At the same time, we have countless cases of people and groups who took a risk, became less rigid, and thrived in states of complexity.

TAKE A GANDER AT CREATIVITY FLOURISHING IN A STATE OF COMPLEXITY

For one of my favorite examples that really illustrates the conditions for creativity we'll explore later on, let's go back to my beloved Newfoundland and Labrador.

What happened during 9/11 in Gander, Newfoundland, is a story that has been told many times before, but I will tell it again because not only does the feat almost defy belief, but every time it is told, new details come to light from the 16,000+ souls who were unexpectedly thrown together that day. For that reason alone, it is a story that will never get old. It beautifully shows how a community embraced overwhelming change and uncertainty during an immense state of complexity and utter chaos and fostered innovation, imagination, and a culture of belonging to create ripples of inspiration that are still felt around the world to this day.

It becomes even more inspirational if you compare the feat achieved by the townsfolk of Gander with how an organization today, bound tightly by its self-inflicted processes and hierarchies, might approach such a situation.

Imagine, if you will, the reaction of any organization, either public or private-sector, being tasked with an operation that would require it to land 42 flights from around the world and host, for about a week, 6,600 people of many different languages and cultures in a small Newfoundland town of 10,000 with only 550 hotel rooms.

Even as a planned event, most organizations today would flat-out refuse. Those willing to take it on would say they required at least two or three years to build new hotels and restaurants and millions in financial backing. They would need consultants, meetings, GANNT charts, processes, and a committee to organize more committees. To add some context, the facilities to house 2,600 athletes during the 2010 Winter Olympics in Whistler, B.C., took almost four years to build and cost, depending on which source you look at, from $500 million to $1 billion.

But on September 11, 2001, the people of Gander had no such opportunity to plan or budget for this unprecedented event that was about to happen. (Consider, too, that this took place before the age of widespread social media communications and its ability to rally and coordinate efforts.) On that morning, this small-town airport on the northeastern tip of North America was designated as the destination for more than three dozen diverted flights to land due to the terrorist attacks in New York and Washington.

Within this extreme state of complexity and chaos, where no one knew what was going to happen next (or even what was happening right now), the people and business communities of the Gander region banded together and took action. Rather than simply react to the complex events, or try to hold on to the status quo, they worked together to reinvent the future.

Gander became the little town that could. Every individual was needed to take part, for it was recognized that *every single individual had leadership skills and talents to offer*. Even the high school students were required to spend all class time volunteering to help with the guests. Guided by radio announcements, residents and businesses quickly gathered up the essentials for their 6,600 unexpected guests: blankets, toothbrushes and toothpaste, soap and shampoo, deodorant, and even socks and underwear.

Next, *they took a strength-based approach*. Instead of looking at the circumstances as a series of problems to be solved, the people involved took a strength-based approach and looked at "what could be." With compassion and grace, they sought not only to meet the physical needs of the stranded passengers but also to bring about emotional comfort, inspiration, and even joy. In doing so, they created a future that, quite unpredictably, brought positivity and profound meaning out of a very tragic situation.

Then, in an extraordinary gesture of generosity, the Gander townsfolk built on this strength-based approach to *create a culture of belonging*. They opened their homes, schools, and churches to the weary and worried passengers, offering hot showers, guest rooms, home-cooked meals, and someone to talk to. They sourced kosher food for an Orthodox Jewish family and found interpreters for those who could not speak English. They even took people on excursions and sightseeing trips, hikes through the forest, and boat cruises around the harbor. The local phone company, Newtel Communications, enabled passengers to call their loved ones and let them know they were safe. Later, in the *Pittsburgh Post-Gazette*, an American passenger described the people of Gander as endlessly cheerful, giving, and kind, dropping everything to make the stranded passengers "feel less isolated and abandoned during those five days of uncertainty."

From this environment, *the conditions were in place for the extraordinary to happen*. Many people expressed that when thinking back on this time, they would never forget the goodness and kindness showered on them from the people of Gander. Passengers cried as they told these stories. The passengers of one flight, Delta 15, even set up a scholarship fund. To date, the fund has paid out more than $1.5 million and assisted more than 135 students in Newfoundland and Labrador.

Given this example, it's easy to see how faculties of vision and creation are needed in states of complexity. But when we consider how different people approach times of inbetweenity or complexity, when one group clings to the past and a second group is only comfortable talking about change instead of taking action, how can we successfully unleash individual and collective imaginative and creative potential so we can all move into the future together?

THE FUTURE LOOKS BRIGHT

As we steer our courses of action through this modern-day state of complexity, there is cause for great optimism. Several bodies of research are revealing a very interesting story about the human condition. We are continuing to learn more about who we are and how each of us can help shape the next stages of our development. We are learning more about what motivates us. We have developed a richer understanding of the nature of intelligence itself. We have greater insights into how we come to learn what we learn. We are starting to understand more about the intricate connections between emotion and cognition in the learning process. And thanks to amazing research made possible by technologies such as MRI, we are gaining deeper insights into the workings of the human brain. This work is bringing into focus a story of human capacity, of human learning, and, ultimately, of human potential.

Simultaneous to this research are visionary people embracing the uncertainties with their imagination and will who have started to draw connections, understandings, and potential patterns that will help us on our individual and collaborative journeys to shape desirable futures.

Sir Ken Robinson (2011), Professor Emeritus of Education, University of Warwick, and renowned creativity expert, is challenging us to transform learning. He says our educational systems were originally created to meet the requirements of the industrial economy. Like several of his peers, he believes we must rethink the current educational structure to make education relevant in today's world.

Another best-selling author and speaker, Daniel Pink (2009), is challenging us to draw on the new understandings of how we learn and how we are motivated and to reshape our organizations in a way that engages and motivates the people within them.

There's also Mihály Csíkszentmihályi (1997), whose work in the field of optimal experience and optimal learning has provided practical insights regarding how to foster environments in which people become attuned to their own creative learning potential.

Then there's Ellen Langer (1997), whose theories about mindfulness and the power of mindful learning show us that especially in times of complexity, the best thing we can do is believe there is more than one answer or correct way of looking at things. This approach of looking at different perspectives injects novelty, surprise, and esthetic into the learning environment.

Organizations are dedicating themselves to this cause. The Imaginative Literacy Program, *founded by Kieran Egan,* has created a website packed with theories, principles, and practical education techniques. The program believes that engaging students' imaginations in learning, and teachers' imaginations in teaching, is crucial to making knowledge in the curriculum vivid and meaningful. Their approach to teaching literacy draws on a sense of story, feelings and images, metaphors and jokes, the sense of wonder, heroes and the exotic, hopes, fears, and passions, and more to engage the imaginations of both teachers and students.

MY FATHER SHOWED ME HOW TO STAND IN THE WIND

We also have countless other examples of everyday people who took a risk and thrived in times of complexity. You may have heard the story of Zita

Cobb who, after retiring from her position as a top executive at JDS Uniphase, moved home to Fogo Island off the coast of Newfoundland and Labrador to help to reignite the economic health of her birthplace. She certainly exemplifies someone who embraces change and views the future as something to be invented. What you may not have heard is the story of her father, Lambert Cobb, from whom Zita appears to have inherited resiliency and foresight.

I was fortunate enough to hear Zita speak during one of our Lead the Way events for the Ottawa-Carleton District School Board. Zita's parents raised seven children in a home without electricity or running water. Her father's family had fished in the region for generations before him.

Lambert Cobb could not read or write and yet, according to Zita, he was a pioneer in education. She explained how until the 1960s, Fogo Island was quite isolated from the rest of the world. Even the island's 10 communities had very little contact with each other. And within each community, schools were under the control of the church, and students were therefore even further divided into Protestant, Catholic, United, and Anglican schools. Multiply that by 10 communities, said Zita, and you have a lot of little schools and not that much education.

So when the inshore fishery came on the verge of economic collapse, Lambert realized that whereas people on the island had lived for 400 years in their own little world, where it didn't really matter much if one couldn't read or write, change was coming and they would have to learn to live in the big world.

Lambert then became an agitator to put all the students, regardless of religion, together in one high school. As a result, Zita's brother Steve was the first Catholic kid to go to a Protestant school—and that was instrumental in the move toward establishing an integrated high school on Fogo Island.

Although Zita Cobb has in many ways become a hero herself, as we discuss later in this book, in her eyes her father was her hero; he was the one who showed her how to "stand in the wind."

HOW DO YOU BEGIN TO MAKE THE EXTRAORDINARY HAPPEN?

It's clear that we as a society have much to gain from innovation, and this time of immense change and complexity sets the perfect stage for a new creative age.

In these first two chapters, I've tried to explain why creativity is so critical right now in this state of complexity. As you continue to read, you can start thinking about how you can map your way into the future and make sense of everything that's going on around you. It's really important to first determine *where you are right now*. You need to gauge how people in your school—or your organization, family, or community—are feeling about and responding to the complexity in their lives. And despite all the great work that's been done by the experts, you will need to do your own work here, because no two individuals, groups, or organizations are alike. That means you'll have to ask some really profound questions and create a culture of trust so people aren't afraid to give you some honest answers.

Remember, too, that you have an opportunity to be a leader here, because there is a close connection among creativity, learning, and leadership. And by leadership, I don't just mean those who are in official leadership positions. *The Wonder Wall* is based on the understanding that everyone can and does exhibit amazing leadership roles in his or her jobs and everyday lives, and it is this type of informal leadership that really defines and fosters the heart, soul, and culture of an organization and can contribute to its progress.

So as you begin, the question you want to ask is *How do you make the extraordinary happen*? How can you help to ignite and harness the creative capacities within people? And there are questions you will want to ask others: What does leadership mean to you? What are the behaviors and characteristics of leadership? What is the ideal definition of leadership? And then ask the most important question: How are you being supported in your leadership capacities? When you get the answers, you'll need to deal with these discussions openly and honestly and start the journey to grow your organization from there.

Stories From the Field

Everybody Is a Teacher

Principal Connie Daymond has seen firsthand the rewards of fostering leadership and creativity at all levels. "My philosophy is everybody is a teacher in the school. Whether you are a chief custodian, an office administrator, a volunteer, a business partner—everybody is a teacher," she told me. "Anyone can come forward with an idea we can work on to make our school a better place."

One inspiring example at her school is the Green Team, which was founded and has flourished under the leadership of chief custodian Josh Rebertz. I snapped this picture of Josh with one of his young protégés one day, and he explained to me what was happening in the photo and how the Green Team works.

"This was a little kindergarten boy who was having difficulties at the beginning of his school life, with various types of behavior problems.

"However, his teacher noticed he really liked to play with keys. Well, I've got hundreds of keys, many of which are no longer in use. So I made him a set of old keys and gave it to his teacher. She kept the keys in her desk and when he had a good day, he got to play with the keys."

Photo courtesy of Josh Rebertz and Katherine Pelletier

Eventually, Josh and the teacher wondered if getting the student to do a bit of work with Josh would further help him.

"To start, I would have him deliver a paper with me. We would go get a paper from the main office and take it to the photocopy room, and at that point I gave him an actual set of keys, and he would open the doors for me that we had to pass through.

"He was very proud of those keys; he wore them around his neck and showed them to everybody. So we started involving him in some little jobs occasionally. We started with sweeping. I took a broom and cut it down to his size, which you can see in the picture. He loved it so much that I did the same thing with a mop. It was great to see him enjoy the cleaning as much as he did. So whenever he had a good week, at 2 o'clock on Friday afternoon, I would go and pick him up, we would go and get the set of keys, and he'd put them around his neck and we'd sweep the halls."

The student began to flourish under Josh's leadership. "He built an amazing amount of confidence. Every time another student saw him in the hallway they would say, 'Oh, what are you doing with Mr. Josh?' And he would say with this big grin, 'Oh, I'm helping him work and clean.' And he would show off his keys."

Today, the "Green Team" concept has expanded throughout the school, working with kids that teachers suggest might need a little guidance or are in need of an outlet.

(Continued)

(Continued)

"We got a great response from the teachers and formed a group of 15 kids to collect recycling. Now we've expanded to 25 kids, working in groups of five, five days a week," says Josh. "The main point is to get the kids a little more involved, to build their teamwork skills and leadership skills. The students really feel great about being part of the team. Last year we even got T-shirts made, and it's a real highlight to see the kids' faces light up when they put on their Green Team shirts."

"Once Josh started to work with the kids, you could see the change almost instantly in some of their behaviors," Connie says. "Learning is also a key benefit. We have kids who would rather work with Josh than do math, so part of the process is to get them to understand that subjects like language and math and social studies are important to Josh's work. Josh really reinforces the connections between what he does in the school to what other people do and the work that they do in their classes."

Connie adds that Josh's leadership is invaluable to the teaching process. "When there was a problem in the classroom, sometimes Josh would be called upon because of the relationship he had built with the student. With Josh, we're building a culture of school teaching, not classroom teaching."

Josh says, "It puts a face to the people that maintain the building. It helps the kids have a little more respect for the space they're in, more respect for each other, and more respect for themselves that they build through their leadership and teamwork roles. If they can take that away from it, that makes it all worthwhile."

Try This!

How do you get an accurate baseline of where leadership stands in your organization? First, don't be afraid to ask the tough questions. Second, ask everyone in the organization for their views and solutions. Solutions and leadership must come from every part of the organization—and from outside of it. Ask *How do you create the conditions to foster an engaged and creative organization*? Then listen to what they have to say. Finally, involve everyone in coming up with solutions and doing something about it.

3 The Imperatives for Creativity

Getting There Is a Three-Way Street

> *"Every man, when he gets quiet, when he becomes desperately*
> *honest with himself, is capable of uttering profound truths. . . .*
> *We are all part of creation, all kings, all poets, all musicians;*
> *we have only to open up, only to discover what is already there."*
>
> —Henry Miller

When I was involved with the Lead the Way campaign with the Ottawa-Carleton District School Board in Canada (which I'll describe in more detail later), we realized that the thousands of people who came to our events had all kinds of ideas and insight about creativity, innovation, and leadership. So we began to tap into their knowledge by inviting them to submit their answers to various questions, including, "What are the conditions under which healthy and creative individuals and organizations flourish?"

This resonated with people, and we received thousands of suggestions over the years, which were all carefully catalogued and analyzed for commonality and patterns. Originally, we had dozens of distinct conditions, ranging from autonomy for teachers to more zest for risk taking.

It was all very fascinating, but we weren't sure how we could possibly apply this wealth of information in a practical manner. The idea of embedding dozens of conditions into a learning environment before we could see creativity flourish sounded exhausting.

You can understand why I wasn't initially that eager to start writing a book about it all. Such a project would certainly become *The Never Ending Story*.

But once I took a few steps back from the project, the bigger picture became clearer to me. There may be dozens, even hundreds, of conditions, but when you look at the end goal, these conditions all serve to support and embed three main imperatives into a culture or environment. It is this three-way street that must be present for creativity to flourish—and you can achieve these imperatives by using the conditions you find most practical and suitable for you to implement in your unique situation.

Imperatives for Creativity

1. Recognize there is a seed of brilliance in everyone.

2. Adopt a strength-based approach.

3. Create cultures of belonging.

Let's go through these in more detail.

Imperative #1: Recognize There Is a Seed of Brilliance in Everyone

On August 6, 2011, I arrived in Britain to visit my mum. As it turns out, it was the same day a number of riots broke out, in which thousands of people across several locations engaged in looting, arson, and violence. (I'm not sure if there is a connection between these two events.)

At that time, my mother lived on the Wirral—a peninsula on the northwest coast of England bordered by the River Mersey to the north (the river made famous in the Mersey beat era by Gerry and the Pacemakers) and the River Dee to the south.

Everyone in Liverpool suspected the riots in London on August 6 would spark copycat riots across the country, and almost certainly in parts of Liverpool. We were not mistaken. What we had not anticipated was that riots would also break out in Birkenhead, only three miles from where my mum lived. This brought the unrest rather uncomfortably close to home.

The civil unrest during that short period was terrifying for the country. Civil society broke down. As I sat there with my mum watching the news on August 10, it was clear that if anyone was in need of emergency services, there would be a long wait.

Later in the week, as things started to calm down, I took a trip to Chester and headed for the bookstore. There I picked up a copy of Michael Caine's new autobiography, *The Elephant to Hollywood*. He is my favorite actor, so it was a nice surprise to see it.

One of the stories he relates in the book pertains to his experiences during the filming of the 2009 action thriller *Harry Brown*. This rather intense movie is set in the Elephant and Castle, a poverty-stricken suburb of East London that's infamous for its gang activity. If you've seen the place, you'll understand what I mean when I say the very architecture of the tenement buildings seems intent on fostering social unrest.

Interestingly, Michael Caine was born into and grew up in the very same suburb. And through this part of his book, he reveals his curiosity as to why he did not follow the path into gang membership—the path taken by so many of the other youth from the Elephant and Castle.

Much of *Harry Brown* was filmed at night, so Caine scouted out the area during the day. While doing so, he began to talk to some of the gangs of youths hanging around the neighborhood. To his astonishment, he gained their trust—and they started to share their stories with him. Caine came to understand that the combination of broken homes, availability of drugs, and the violence that accompanies the gang lifestyle all contributed to the complexity of the lives of these youth and laid the groundwork for the paths they found themselves on.

It became clear to Caine that although he had also lived a life of financial poverty, only 1,000 yards from the monstrous blocks of flats that formed the setting for the movie, he had had the stability of a loving family. This was simply not the case for many of the boys he was speaking with.

Perhaps most significantly, he realized these kids had nothing to do. They had nowhere to go. No sense of belonging. Caine (2011), at least, as he explains, had Clubland, a youth club and drama classes, "and that was where I found the thing I wanted to do more than anything else, the thing that, in the end, set me on my future course" (p. 346).

At Clubland, Caine was blessed to find the person who helped shape the course of his life: the Reverend Jimmy Butterworth. He believes that without him he would likely never have made it out of the Elephant and Castle.

SEEDS OF BRILLIANCE CAN BLOOM IN UNEXPECTED PLACES

So what does this have to do with the first imperative of recognizing there is a seed of brilliance in everyone? Well, consider that many people might sympathize with this gang of youths and their troubled backgrounds and may even support providing funding or better housing or the like in an attempt to alleviate the problem. And that's great. But few would have viewed these gang members as people with brilliance and leadership abilities, people you would want to hire. Yet that is exactly what the director of *Harry Brown*, Daniel Barber, did. Barber noticed some of the young men watching as they filmed at night and decided to hire them to be in the movie.

Caine (2011) thought this would present the bold director with some considerable headaches. But then he watched, amazed, as the young men became fascinated and engaged with what they were doing:

> As I watched Daniel directing these kids, it dawned on me that here was proof of what was lacking in their lives. They were doing something they really wanted to do, they were interested enough to want to know how to do it well, and they were responding to an authority figure who knew what he was talking about and was treating them with the dignity and respect their lives were lacking. By take 5, they were completely into it and making their own suggestions—I loved watching the way their confidence grew by the minute. (p. 348)

AN AUTO BODY EXPERIENCE

Just as we need to look for potential in these troubled youths, we need to see the potential brilliance in our students with talents in diverse areas and find a way to fulfill them. I learned this firsthand several years ago when I had an accident and visited the local auto body shop. As I was chatting with the young man at the front desk, a voice called out from an adjoining room.

"Is that a limey accent I hear?"

"Yes, it is," I retorted. "And I would recognize the dulcet tones of an Irishman anywhere."

Out came the owner, whose name I soon learned was Roy.

Roy and I then engaged in banter for several minutes, the form of banter in which only the English and the Irish can engage. Eventually, when we had run out of banter, Roy asked me what I did. I explained I worked for the school board. When he asked me for a more specific job description, I said I was a superintendent.

"Aha, one of the high-ups," he said. And then his manner became quite serious.

"Follow me," he demanded.

I dutifully followed Roy to the back, where he opened the door to the workshop. There were quite a number of young people engaged in various forms of bodywork.

"What do you see there?" Roy asked me.

"I see young people working hard at their jobs."

"Do they seem to be engaged in what they're doing?"

"They do, indeed," I replied.

"But most of them didn't experience that in their school lives. The system did not help them; in fact, I would say you failed them."

"Pardon?"

"You failed them."

I was tempted to jokingly ask Roy if this was some new and creative customer engagement strategy but decided against it as the subject was clearly important to him. He was quite wound up!

"These young kids have all sorts of talents and abilities—but they aren't the types of abilities they got to experience in the school system. The system didn't serve them well."

Roy then went on to explain that for years, he and some of his colleagues had been trying to partner with individual schools, school boards, and colleges to establish apprenticeship or co-op programs and had met with roadblocks and barriers. He and his colleagues knew there are many kids in the system who fall through the cracks.

"It's not that they don't have abilities; it's not that they are stupid," Roy explained. "It's that they have interests and abilities that don't fit the mold of the education system. And so they either quit or fail."

Roy's frustration was that he knew there were opportunities in his industry that could help transform these students' lives, engaging them in experiences that would resonate with their interests and their passions. Through partnerships, Roy and his colleagues wanted to reach some of these kids and offer them opportunities not offered in the system.

I'm never one to turn down an opportunity for a partnership. Two months later, I invited Roy and a colleague to come to our Lead the Way leadership conference to express their concerns and offer possible solutions.

Whereas school systems do strive to offer wonderful programs and learning opportunities for all manner of learners, including apprenticeship training and co-op placements, we need to heed Roy's words that we must look for the brilliance and abilities that students possess within, rather than assessing them on abilities we deem them not to have. We must be constantly nimble and fluid in challenging ourselves to offer opportunities and partnerships customized to meet the needs of all our learners.

WANT A SMARTER ORGANIZATION? RECOGNIZE INDIVIDUAL BRILLIANCE

As you may have heard, the theory that humans use only 10 percent of their brains is untrue, and the majority of people do, in fact, use all parts of their gray matter. (Although my wife has politely pointed out that "majority" doesn't mean "everyone," and I shouldn't be too quick to assume which category I fall into.)

But whereas most of us are relieved we're not wasting 90 percent of our brainpower, we regularly do so in our classrooms, organizations, and communities. We need to broaden our definitions of what potential or success looks like. I'll discuss this more later, but I believe most companies fail to engage 90 percent of their organization's brainpower below the executive floor. Imagine how much more creative and innovative a company could be if it tapped into that brilliance. As educators, one way we can help organizations get into the practice of seeing leadership and creative capacities in every individual is to start by doing it in our classrooms and schools.

I'd heard some years ago that if you ask a kindergarten class which of them is creative, all hands will go up, but by middle school, only a few will claim to be creative—most will point to the kids that excel in art or music or writing.

I wanted to see if this was true, so I tried it myself at several schools. Not only did the students react exactly as predicted, but interestingly, some teachers followed suit!

Imagine that. By the age of 13, students have already begun to point away from themselves, to be blind to their own creative potential.

WE NEED TO DEMYSTIFY CREATIVITY

Part of the reason people don't see themselves (and most others) as being creative is that we're not quite sure what creativity is, or what it means, or where and how it can be applied.

If we want to foster creativity and innovation throughout our schools and organizations, we must first engage people in demystifying the concept of creativity. If we want people to see their potential, we must understand creativity lies within all of us, across all intelligences and skill sets, and all sectors, from architecture to zoology, from plumbing to neuroscience.

For too long, creativity has been associated almost solely with the arts or perhaps extremely clever scientists. But by making creativity relevant to people—to all people—we can make a mind-set shift. Individuals can understand creativity isn't just something *others* have and can begin reflecting on their own imaginative capacities and their own creative uniqueness and potential.

We encouraged this mind-set shift at the Ottawa-Carleton District School Board. In 2008, we brought together 50 people from our community who were respected by those around them for fostering cultures that were open, honest, and trusting; people who were known to draw on the capacities of every person. These leaders came from all sectors, including the arts, trades, business, police services, management, volunteer organizations, sports, and many others. We then sat down with this group, along with a group of principals, vice principals, teachers, and community representatives, and asked them to talk about the importance of creativity in their personal and professional lives. Starting with personal perspectives, we wanted to begin shifting people's understanding of imagination, creativity, and innovation.

At that initial meeting, we had no idea we were embarking on a journey to creativity and leadership that would span several years and draw in thousands of people from around the world. A snapshot report of that journey, outlined in *Unleashing Potential, Harnessing Possibilities: An Odyssey of Creativity, Innovation, & Critical Thinking*, published by the Ottawa-Carleton District School Board (2012), attracted attention and interest not only from other school boards, businesses, and organizations but also from the premier of Ontario, the provincial government of British Columbia, the National Creativity Network, the American Imagination Summit, and the World Creativity Forum in Oklahoma, where I was on the expert panel with Sir Ken Robinson. I and other participants in this initiative have also been invited to speak to more than 50 audiences, from a range of sectors, across Canada and the United States and as far away as Argentina and Australia.

Clearly, the idea that everyone has creative capacities resonates with people.

I fully credit the success of the Lead the Way campaign on its foundational belief that everyone had ideas and capabilities to offer. Once you embed that belief across your school system or organization, then it's quite easy to start acting on it and reaping the benefits of that creative brilliance. That not only benefits society but also individual students who can enjoy engaging their inner talents and reaching their full potential.

Imperative #2: Adopt a Strength-Based Approach

"Knowing what is and knowing what can be are not the same thing."

—Ellen Langer

Consider the annual leadership planning session. This exercise is often held at a remote wilderness retreat. They say it's held in these settings far from civilization so we won't be distracted, but I firmly believe these densely forested locations are chosen to discourage us from trying to escape. I'm sure the owners of Alcatraz could turn a tidy profit if they opened the facility up for corporate meetings.

Typically, once you and your coworkers arrive at the Hungry Grizzlies Hotel, you're herded into an airless gathering place where a giant whiteboard stares you down from the front of the room. Along one wall, an array of sandwiches and soft drinks is provided. You wonder if you should cram a few seasoned chicken wraps into your pockets. The scent might attract the grizzlies, but you're not sure when you'll get to eat again.

You take your seats at the round tables, all facing each other, and a grim-faced team leader stands up and tells you how much less money you'll have to spend this year than last. Sacrifices must be made, and you're all handed markers (appropriately called "Sharpies") and tasked with *solving problems* by slashing various programs to death. By the end of it all, everyone is disheartened and wondering if getting lost in the wilderness is really such a terrible way to go.

Too often, and especially in challenging times or states of complexity, our lives, schools, and organizations are entrenched in deficit models of thinking and acting. Much of what we do, and our collective creative effort, is directed at *solving problems*, of which we seem to have an endless supply.

If we are really serious about fostering creative, healthy, and dynamic learning cultures that engage the diverse and varied abilities of our people, then we need to think and act from a strength-based perspective.

Ask yourself, "What are the amazing possibilities we want to achieve within the organization?" and "How are we going to make that happen?"

Second, when dealing with individuals or groups, what's the magic we want to reveal? How are we going to achieve that?

Many of our organizations, as we've just described, get stuck in a deficit mode of thinking and acting. They operate from a problem-solving perspective, believing the pathway forward is best served by identifying problems and then setting in place processes to solve those problems. We ask, "What are our problems? How do we fix them?"

Well, let me tell you a secret. In today's state of complexity, if you want to ask people to identify problems and write them down, there will be no shortage. By the end of this process, the blackboard or whiteboard disappears behind the deluge of problems identified and people in the room are left exhausted and depressed.

Problem solving is an essential part of life, and it has an important place in an overall strategy. What we need to do, though, is flip our perspective from a deficit to a strength-based mind-set. Move away from thinking about what you are lacking, or what you want, to focusing on what you have and what you can get, including from partnerships. We need to look at what we've got and think positively about how we can best use it.

Ask "What are the amazing possibilities we want to achieve in our organization?" and "How are we going to get there?" and you will accomplish four things.

1. You'll flip a negative mind-set to a positive one.

The process now becomes a journey into possibility. This fosters a culture of positive thinking and learning that empowers people, groups, and organizations to make a strength-based approach a practice—and I mean *practice* as a verb. It is a cultural shift that has to occur over and over again to become innate, instinctive, and woven into the very fabric of the classroom or organization. It contributes in a critical way to the fostering of creative learning.

2. This cultural shift provides an opportunity to flatten the hierarchy of your organization in two key ways:
   - As you explore the possibilities and pathways forward, your thinking will be enriched by consulting with the people who actually do the work. In this way, the learning culture of the organization becomes more inclusive, as ideas are expected to emerge from anywhere, not just from the top of the hierarchy.
   - It redefines how you look at leadership, a shift from positional authority to personal leadership. This doesn't negate the importance of formal leadership—it simply makes it better. And it prepares the next generation of leadership and enhances and expands successional planning across the organization.

3. A strength-based approach promotes new ideas, collaboration, and cooperation, rather than pitting colleagues against each other to compete for scarce resources or budgets.

4. This process promotes creativity by encouraging the participants to focus *outside* the problem's parameters to find solutions.

Step-by-Step Guide for How to Solve Problems

On the Hunt for Problems

Some organizations make focusing on problems an integral part of their operations and processes—they have regularly scheduled problem-solving meetings, wherein individuals can bring forth the problems they hunt for throughout the week. Some provide their teams with step-by-step guides on how to solve problems. Here's an example of a quick step-by-step guide provided to employees. You may have seen a similar version.

What Problems Have You Identified?

1. Keep a pad of paper handy to list all the problems you come across in your daily work, or log them on your phone. Include the things that bother, annoy, or irritate not only you but also your coworkers and our customers. Note how the problem affects productivity, profits, employee morale, or customer satisfaction.

2. In your opinion, what is causing this problem? (Processes? Lack of training? Lack of resources? Human error? Client error? Technology malfunction?)

3. What is the full impact of the problem? (What new problems does it create? List all that apply.)

4. When is the problem occurring? How does it affect decisions/actions up and down the process chain? What impact does it have on the rest of the process?

5. Which departments or individuals are involved with the problem? (List all that apply.)

6. How does the problem affect other stakeholders and our relationships with them? Employees? Customers?

7. How does the problem affect our brand and reputation?

8. What are the consequences if this problem is not resolved in a timely manner?

9. Please bring your notes to the weekly meeting to be discussed.

Try This!

Muscle up Your Students' Strength-Based Skills

Think of when you have taken a strength-based approach. How can you build on this with your classroom? Try this to give your students firsthand experience on how taking a strength-based approach changes everything!

Divide the students into groups and announce you are going to do a simple arts and crafts project, perhaps gluing together cut-out pieces of construction paper to form a specified animal such as a peacock. (Older students could be given a simple construction project, such as a birdhouse.)

Show the students a picture or model of what the finished piece should look like and then hand out the various material pieces and tools each group will need in a kit or box (precut pieces of construction paper and glue or pieces of wood, screwdriver, and screws) and tell them to get started.

Then sit back and watch the fun begin—because unbeknown to the students, no group will have all the materials or tools necessary to complete the project. Some will have no tail feathers to complete the peacock, others will have one leg and no beak. One group will have no glue. The students may also find random objects in their kit that have nothing to do with construction-paper peacocks—a ball of yarn, an empty egg carton, a pinecone, or a Ping-Pong ball. For the older students, one group might have six walls and no roof; another group might have screws, but they're the wrong size. One group might have no birdhouse materials at all but a framed photo of a cat and a rubber chicken instead. Some might get instructions for a different outcome, such as a recipe for making oatmeal cookies.

Allow the students a minute or two to exclaim about the hopelessness of their situation, then ask them to list all the problems they have with trying to complete the project with the materials and tools they've been given. Write them on the board, if desired.

Ask them how they feel after listing all the problems. Frustrated? Optimistic? Motivated?

Now turn the tables on them. Tell them, "You've focused on all the problems and things you can't do with what you've been given. Now let's turn it around. What are some things you *can* do? Focus on how you can take what you have and create something extraordinary; to see what you have not for what it is but what it *could* be."

(Continued)

(Continued)

Then let them go at it. Your groups may even figure out on their own that their "something extraordinary" will have even more creative possibilities if they form partnerships with other groups, exchanging and borrowing tools, materials, and even the knowledge and talents of individuals. If they don't, this is also a perfect opportunity to teach them the value of community partnerships.

You'll no doubt get some very interesting and creative results, some of which may not even turn out to be peacocks or birdhouses at all.

After the projects are complete, ask the students some key questions:

Compared to when you were listing problems to be solved, how did you feel when using a strength-based approach? In which situation did you feel your brain was more engaged? In which situation did you learn more? What about the results? How did results differ between the problem-focused approach and the strength-based approach? In what other aspects of your life can you use a strength-based approach? What are some current challenges the world faces? If a strength-based approach was applied, how might the challenge be differently approached?

Throughout the year, make a point of encouraging students to apply a strength-based approach to the challenges they come across, including looking for favorable partnerships and other resources wherever possible. Ask them on a regular basis, "Have you thought about taking a strength-based approach to that? Is there a resource or partner who could help with a solution or guide you toward your goal?"

Don't forget to encourage your colleagues and the school and community at large to apply a strength-based approach whenever possible. And please don't hesitate to share your insights or project photos on my website at petergamwell.com.

HOW A MIND-SET SHIFT CHANGES EVERYTHING

Once the strength-based model becomes entrenched, it draws the morale, motivation, and momentum of the entire organization into an upward spiral and a culture of possibility.

Interestingly, considering how people react to times of inbetweenity and times of rapidly changing complexity, it's natural for people to try to assert more control over the way they approach both challenges and opportunities. This is certainly one of the reasons we find standardized curriculum and testing valuable and appealing.

But a strength-based mind-set, as I mentioned earlier that Carol Dweck observed, can take us beyond the "what is" that these tests measure and help us achieve "what could be." Imagine how students and employees would react if, instead of only telling them "Here's what you are, according to our standardized tests," we added, "Let's also think about what you could become" according to our belief that you have great capabilities beyond what these tests measure. And we can take this approach not only with individuals and groups but also companies, organizations, and communities.

HOW CAN WE VIEW OUR STUDENTS THROUGH A STRENGTH-BASED MODEL?

To examine this further, let's take our approach to education as another example.

If an educational organization truly values the full range of its students' capacities, then this approach will manifest itself not only throughout the school board but across the greater district and community. Under the strength-based paradigm, students' unique capacities will be identified and opportunities will be sought for them to experience and grow in these areas of interest, using partnerships from across multiple sectors in the greater community. Students benefit through the recognition of their particular abilities and feel invigorated as they get to experience success in areas of strength.

This is not to say we don't also need to look at those areas where a student is struggling. We must identify challenges and draw on the very best research and educational assessment tools at our disposal to ensure we do all we can to help students. But this must be done in the context of an education system that focuses on a student's personal strengths as well, whatever they may be. We can't become so myopically focused on their challenges we never see or pay attention to the abilities they have. Parents often say, "You tell me all about the problems my child has, but we see her amazing abilities, too. Why do you never talk about her abilities?"

A strength-based approach will also help students understand where their strengths lie, which will in turn inform their decisions regarding any postsecondary education or goals. According to Cecilia Capuzzi Simon (2012), "Some students go to college knowing exactly what they want to do. But most don't. At Penn State, 80 percent of freshmen—even those who have declared a major—say they are uncertain about their major, and half will change their minds after they declare, sometimes more than once."

Beyond math and language skills, we need to develop the skills employers need for today's competitive global marketplace. For example, according to Martha C. White (2013), various studies show that a wide margin of employers identify skills such as "communication, critical thinking, creativity and collaboration" as the biggest knowledge gap students have today. White's article references the annual Global Talent Shortage survey, conducted by Manpower Group, as stating that one in five employers worldwide can't find people to fill positions due to a lack of soft skills.

PUT A STRENGTH-BASED APPROACH TO WORK AND GET CREATIVITY TO BOOT

Imagine how much different your next staff meeting, planning session, or PTA meeting might be if it was approached from a strength-based perspective—an opportunity to sit down and say, "Here's what we have to start with. What is the ideal vision? What great things can we achieve with this over the next twelve months? How can we align resources (perhaps even find new resources), funding, and partnerships to achieve the extraordinary?"

By the end of the meeting, the positivity of the process means most will leave feeling emotionally recharged and positive, still thinking of new possibilities and solutions, and will take that feeling and attitude back to the classroom with them.

In fact, I promise you that if you try this strength-based approach at your next team meeting, you will feel how the energy in the room shifts. This powerful step moves people from a negative space to a positive one, completely reframing their mind-set of thinking and acting. It's that simple.

To realize creative potential, we need to think and act from a strength-based mind-set. We need to see our people, our students, and even our organizations as miracles to be embraced, rather than problems to be solved. Shifting to a strength-based mind-set will have a profound impact on the culture of an organization, challenging people to embrace enveloping uncertainties—to imagine novel and interesting ways to achieve more within their sphere of influence.

To help make this mind-set shift in our individual and organizational thinking, we need to identify the types of conditions that will foster creativity and enable optimal learning to take place.

HOW TO START FOSTERING A STRENGTH-BASED APPROACH

One of the best things about taking a strength-based approach is that it is probably the easiest imperative to implement to foster creativity. Simply take the deficit-based approach individuals and organizations have often been trained to follow and turn it upside down. When conducting your next meeting, whether it's about student progress or the budget, consider asking some of these example questions:

> What can we do to make the extraordinary happen? If you could imagine your ideal school place or workplace world, what would it look like?

> How would our students, employees, and greater community benefit from this extraordinary ideal? Are there others who would benefit?

> What resources, funds, talents, skills, and knowledge do we already have available to work with?

> Are there resources, funds, talents, skills, and knowledge we have but are unaware of? How can we attract more diversity and inclusivity to our project? Do we know people within or outside our organization with whom we could share resources, get funding, or collaborate with?

> Looking at our students, what are their strengths? Is there a way we can harness these strengths and help them grow? Could we even use the students' strengths, passions, and interests to help them understand and embrace other subject material?

> If there are obstacles, how can we overcome them? How can we get more funding, if needed? More space? More people involved? What are some ways we could get the same benefits but on a smaller scale?

> How can we help drum up awareness, enthusiasm, energy, and collaboration for our extraordinary ideal? How do we make everyone involved with our project feel welcome and comfortable sharing their ideas and talents?

Depending on your organization and what your situation and extraordinary ideals involve, you may come up with several other questions to foster a strength-based approach.

Anne Teutsch, a parent, saw the value of the strength-based approach firsthand. In Ottawa, Canada, she was heavily involved with school councils throughout her children's school years, as well as serving as the chair for the Ottawa-Carleton Assembly of School Councils and as a parent representative on several school board committees.

"It's too easy for changes like school closures and realigning resources to cause stresses between various stakeholders, along with a subsequent erosion of trust and negative energy that is very draining," says Anne. "I always tried to encourage working together because we're all here for the same reason: getting the best education for the kids."

Anne found that taking a strength-based approach—let's look at our strengths and what we can do—built a more positive energy and a synergy among the groups. "You feel good about what you're doing so it's a huge morale booster," she says. "Plus, knowing you're being respected and listened to, and hearing their side of the story too, helps build bridges and collaboration across communities."

Imperative #3: Create Cultures of Belonging

I was once told, quite bluntly, that I needed to kill the Care Bears.

It's not because I have a side gig as a stuffed-animal hitman, although I admit beating the stuffing out of those singing teddies does hold a certain appeal for me. It's simply a common reaction I get when I talk about creating cultures of belonging.

Living in a time of complexity and in an increasingly hectic, competitive world, where organizations prioritize productivity and measurability and scalable efficiencies, and control above all else, focusing on "creating a culture of belonging" sounds decidedly unbusinesslike to some, if not downright silly. How are we going to improve test scores and turn the economy around and compete in the global market if we're all holding hands around a campfire, singing *Kumbaya*?

I couldn't fault the colleague who advised me to snuff out my ideas about the power of belonging, for she had my best interests at heart. She feared I'd never be taken seriously in the stern-minded fields of education and business.

"People want to know how they can get results or increase their bottom line, Peter. I'm sure cultures of belonging are all very nice to have, but being concerned about people's emotions just isn't a priority."

A few months later, I received a text message at 2:17 in the morning. It was short and to the point.

"Peter, don't kill the Care Bears. I get it now. It's ALL about the Care Bears."

RESEARCH SHOWS EMOTIONS DRIVE LEARNING

After the sun had risen, I asked my formerly murderous-minded colleague what had led to her change of heart. There were a number of factors.

For the results-driven side of her, she had learned emotions actually play a key role in learning and organizational success. Part of this is common sense: If a student feels excluded, anxious, or inadequate, he or she is less likely to become engaged in participating or what is being taught or commit the lessons to memory. We've all had the experience of reading a document and then realizing we can't remember a word of it, because our minds have been engaged with some worry or fear.

As more evidence, recent cognitive research shows the brain, particularly the limbic system, physically shuts down the ability to learn or store new information when negative emotions are present. From an evolutionary standpoint, this makes sense. When faced with a situation or perception that evokes fear or anger, the brain feels the need to focus on a flight-or-fight response—there's no room for learning a second language or dissecting an algebra equation.

In fact, fear and anxiety can even make you forget something you've already learned. If you've ever "blanked out" during a test, you've experienced this phenomenon yourself.

Conversely, associating a task with feelings of enjoyment or contentment helps drive attention and feelings of competence and self-esteem. Positive emotions prepare the brain for learning.

For these reasons, considering emotions in the classroom can help enable and enhance student learning. And in this time of complexity it's especially crucial because so many of our students are increasingly dealing with depression, anxiety, and stress.

But back to the reprieved Care Bears. There was one more reason my colleague came to value cultures of belonging. It came to her after she had read about the deeply moving impacts and transformations that cultures of belonging have had on the students, individuals, and groups that I've worked with over the years.

"It is simply the right and compassionate thing to do," she said. "Creating those cultures of belonging is what makes life meaningful. It's the stuff money can't buy. As the human race, what are we doing it all for, if not for that?"

STABILIZING EMOTIONS THROUGH CULTURES OF BELONGING

The challenge with emotions, of course, is that they are an integral part of life. We can't make everyone perpetually happy, and we can't eradicate all feelings of sadness, anger, or fear. Nor would we want to. Dealing with these emotions and their related events are learning experiences in themselves and an essential part of the human experience. As human beings, we need to embrace the full range of our emotions.

So how can we help students better learn then, considering all students will and should experience negative emotions sometimes? And how can we help the most vulnerable, those who are going through tough challenges and those who virtually live in a perpetual world of negativity?

To me, the answer is not to try to control emotions (remember people feel a need to control in times of complexity) but to create cultures of belonging where students feel a sense of calm, a sense of safety, and a sense that there are people there who care about them. In this emotional haven, they may experience sadness and other "negative" emotions (and should not be discouraged from doing so). But with embedded support, they will learn effective and productive ways to deal with these emotions, giving them self-confidence, resilience, coping mechanisms, and the ability to find solutions. They will also experience hope and belonging and emotions that will help them to learn.

As my colleague mentioned, there is also a greater goal and a greater good in creating these environments of belonging. It's about dignity and humanity.

This was recently brought home to me when I was attending a school event and a young teacher approached me. His name was Jason Whiting, and he wanted to tell me a story. What he said brought tears to my eyes and exemplified why cultures of belonging are so imperative.

Jason explained he was the soccer coach for the Canadian Deaf National Team. He got involved partly because both his parents are deaf, and his first language is sign language. But what really convinced him to coach the team was the story that a father of one of the players told him—about what happens when cultures of belonging are not present.

"I was talking to these soccer players who desperately needed a coach, and being deaf, they could really benefit from a coach that could actually speak their language," says Jason. "But I have three kids, and it's a big commitment."

Then one of the fathers took Jason aside. "The story he told me totally changed my life. He said that he had played soccer as a kid too, he was a 13-year-old who was deaf, playing with hearing kids, and he was doing great.

"He was actually one of the better players on the team, banging in goals all the time; he even scored the winner for the finals. They had the year-end team party, and he felt great, that he was adapting in the hearing world.

"A couple of months later, he went with his father to a Maple Leafs hockey game. And he looks across the arena, and he sees one of his soccer teammates. So he signs to his dad, 'Look, there's my buddy over there.' And then he looks closer and he sees another one of his teammates, and then another. The whole team is there. Except for him. And he was just gutted.

"This is a 45-year-old man, in tears, telling me this story that happened decades ago. It still hurt that much."

The father asked Jason if he would coach the team. Jason's response was immediate. "Yes. Oh, yes."

A couple of years later, Jason's team made it to the Pan American games for the deaf, where they beat the host team of Venezuela to claim a spot in the Olympics for the deaf.

"When our player scored the winning goal at the top of the box, they all came and jumped on me; it was everyone coming together. We went to dinner that night, and these guys still hang out with each other now, some of them went back to university, some are traveling the world, some have just wanted to better their lives. Otherwise they would have just gone through the motions and not had that rich learning."

The assistant coach for the team, by the way, was also deaf and a teacher for a fourth-grade class of hearing students.

STILL WATERS IN A STORM

One of the most inspiring role models and mentors I've met in creating environments of belonging is Stephen Haff, founder of Still Waters in a Storm. Formerly a teacher in New York City's public school system, in the troubled neighborhood of Bushwick, Brooklyn, Stephen created Still Waters as "a sanctuary of learning." Indeed, one of the first things he asks of participants at the beginning of each session is for calm.

The classes are free, supported by donations. To explain how Still Waters works, Stephen says, "All of our classes are structured the same way. We study a text, write, then take turns reading our writing out loud and listening to each other. The writing is done in English, Spanish, Latin, or musical notation.

"After each reading, the group responds, not by judging or grading or liking or disliking, but by saying what we noticed, what we felt, what we related to, and by asking questions that encourage fullness and precision of expression.

"The basic ritual is everybody writes, about anything, in any style, adults and children side by side. Then everybody listens to each person read what they've written. That's all. This reverential listening turns lives around, and that is the basis for our work."

Still Waters also has a music program where children are taught to compose original music, as well as Latin classes focused on translating Cicero, Catullus, and Vergil. The program has attracted much positive attention, and close to a hundred famous authors, poets, artists, and musicians have offered their services to help the children find their peace, their voice, and their personal creativity.

I asked Stephen to share his story and the story of Still Waters in a Storm for this book. Here is what he told me:

After seven years of internalizing the various types of violence in the school where I was teaching, the daily physical fights among the students, the power struggles, a harsh regimen of standardized, high-stakes testing, and the violence done to many students on the streets and in their homes, I burned out and had a massive mental breakdown.

Photo courtesy of Stephen Haff

Two children pore over their writing outside Still Waters.

After I recovered, I wanted to continue teaching and stay in touch with my students, so I invited former students to come to my apartment in the neighborhood on Saturdays, to write, to read our writings aloud, and to listen to each other. No tests, no pressure, no critique of the writing, just a chance to be heard, and heard with compassion.

I, too, needed to be heard. I was beginning to build a place that would take care of me as well as the kids. This group grew rapidly, as the students brought their friends, their siblings, even their own young children.

Eventually, friends of mine made it possible to rent a storefront room in Bushwick. I had the room renovated, including a huge window right there on the sidewalk. I didn't want us to be removed from the life of the street.

We never advertised Still Waters. Families walk by and look in the window and ask what's happening. When they find out that we practice reading and writing with all ages, they're very grateful to be included, as they are all recent Spanish-speaking immigrants living in poverty, trying heroically to secure any opportunity for their children. We presently serve more than 60 families, and we have a waiting list of more than 200 families.

People return to Still Waters because it answers a personal and social need, beyond improving their scores on tests at school. It's the need to understand and be understood. I believe we are wired to live in a tribe or village, all ages together, everyone caring for everyone. It feels right for six-year-olds to be sitting beside 12-year-olds, listening to each other. It's safe and reassuring that everyone's together. Our one rule is, "Everyone listens to everyone." Most people, especially children, don't have a place to go where people will listen without judgment or agenda. They find that here. Everyone has a right to beauty, regardless of their ability to pay for it.

This calm, this culture of belonging created at Still Waters, does indeed foster the learning process. Stephen has introduced special reading projects where children as young as seven are reading *Paradise Lost* and *Paradise Regained*, and they are not only understanding the stories but loving the experience.

ANCHORING PEOPLE TO THE COMMUNITY

Another inspiring mentor who creates cultures of belonging is Zita Cobb, who shared her story and rich insight with me. Zita was once one of the highest-paid female executives in North America. She retired in 2001, and after spending a few years traveling, returned to her home of Fogo Island, which is located in the beautiful province of Newfoundland and Labrador.

As I mentioned previously in the story about her father, Lambert Cobb, Zita and her six siblings grew up in a three-room house, with no running water or electricity. When the inshore cod fishery collapsed, her father set fire to his boat and, like so many, moved to the mainland. But Zita had returned often to visit over the years, and the pull to come back to Fogo Island increased with each visit.

When she came back after her traveling, she found the island in decline—a dwindling population and homes and workplaces long since abandoned. It dawned on her that sometimes "you don't know what you've got 'til it's gone." And what had been lost here was a community of belonging.

Zita knew the people of the island had incredible gifts: knowledge and understanding of the land and sea; a ferocious, determined spirit born of the hardships of surviving on an Atlantic island; and breathtaking craftsmanship and artistry.

Why not take those seeds of brilliance and by using a strength-based approach and fostering a culture of belonging, lay the foundation for an environment of creativity and innovation?

With this in mind, Zita and two of her brothers, Anthony and Alan, created the Shorefast Foundation, a registered charity. A symbol of the area's heritage, a shorefast is the line and mooring used to attach a cod trap to the shore. For Zita, it symbolized something more: how community and culture are firmly tied to a place of origin, creating a solid foundation of belonging on which to build an island renaissance.

The Shorefast Foundation seeks to help ensure a resilient economic and cultural future for Fogo Island, and their model may hold learnings for other small places. Shorefast has established three social businesses on Fogo Island, including the world-renowned Fogo Island Inn. Any surpluses from Shorefast's social businesses are redirected back to the charity and reinvested in future initiatives. There is no private gain. Shorefast also operates a series of charitable programs, including the Fogo Island Arts artists-in-residence program, as well as a number of academic residencies.

Today, tiny, nearly forgotten Fogo Island, one of the four corners of the earth according to the Flat Earth Society, has become a thriving international tourist destination. It has flourished with a world-renowned artists-in-residence program and boasts a 29-room, five-star inn. The inn, by the way, was

Photo courtesy of Bent René Synnevåg

furnished entirely by local crafts-men and residents, who were collaborators in the overall development of the project.

For *The Wonder Wall*, I contacted Zita and asked her what we need to do to foster creative organizations. Her response clearly points to the need to establish cultures of belonging.

Zita advises, "Slow down; don't rush into decisions. Involve as many of the people that are connected to the issue as possible. Ask them, 'What do you think?' Reach a perspective and put it out to the group again. Keep asking, 'How can we do this better? How can we do this differently? What would our customers want us to do? What would the community want?' Ask questions that will produce answers which represent the needs of all of the people impacted by the decision."

Within those cultures of belonging, Zita also talks about flattening hierarchies, a key condition for fostering creative environments. She says, "Reduce strict hierarchies and involve all of the people impacted by an issue. For example, at the Inn, we have a daily operations meeting that includes a wide variety of staff members. We usually have the coordinators for each department attend, but if they can't attend, another representative from that department can attend in their place.

"The key is getting all the different department perspectives together, not just certain staff members. In this way, different voices are able to be heard and as many voices as possible are heard. Indeed, these are big meetings with lots of voices involved. But that's what it takes to get the right outcome, and it's well worth doing."

Zita says that using ABCD, or asset-based community development, has been an important part of Shorefast's journey. This involves asking strength-based questions regarding the community and culture you want to create: "What do we have? What do we know? What do we love? What do we miss? What can we do about it?"

And just as many experts are advising of the need to teach the whole child, Zita believes that seeing the world as a whole helps us to learn and create cultures of belonging. "In general, I believe that creativity lies in wholeness. In *A Guide for the Perplexed*, E. F. Schumacher [1978] wrote that every human being should wake in the morning and try to see the world as whole. All of the answers we seek and generative material live in surprising places; sometimes you have to look sideways or up or down because the answers are rarely in the obvious places. Whole thinking helps with this and is the key to creative thinking."

AN ABORIGINAL PERSPECTIVE: HOW BELONGING PROMOTES LEARNING

To gain an Aboriginal perspective on cultures of belonging, I spoke to Dr. Martin Brokenleg. Martin is a cofounder of the Circle of Courage and a consultant for Reclaiming Youth International, providing training worldwide for individuals who work with youth at risk.

The Circle of Courage is a model of positive youth development that Martin (1990), along with coauthors Larry Brendtro and Steve Van Bockern, first described in their book *Reclaiming Youth at Risk*. The model integrates Native American philosophies of child-rearing, the heritage of early pioneers in education and youth work, and contemporary resilience research.

The Circle of Courage is based in four universal growth needs of children: belonging, mastery, independence, and generosity. The very first need, belonging, is described thus:

> In Native American and First Nations cultures, significance was nurtured in communities of belonging. Lakota anthropologist Ella Deloria described the core value of belonging in these simple words: "Be related, somehow, to everyone you know." Treating others as kin forges powerful social bonds that draw all into relationships of respect. Theologian Marty observed that throughout history the tribe, not the nuclear family, always ensured the survival of the culture. Even if parents died or were not responsible, the tribe was always there to nourish the next generation. (Chase, 2015)

That belonging comes first of the four needs is by design.

"This is a critical message for you to get across, the importance of belonging," Martin confirms.

Martin explains that there is consilience with the importance of belonging in the model outlined in the Circle of Courage and other extensive research done on the subject.

"When different researchers using different techniques arrive at the same conclusion, you have consilience," Martin says. "The Search Institute, which is probably the premier research facility agency in North America, used a computer analysis to figure out what helps kids to be successful. They came up with 40 developmental assets, which you can see on their website, and belonging looms the largest."

Unfortunately, Dr. Brokenleg believes that in this frantic-paced world, this time of complexity, we are losing opportunities to create spaces of belonging.

"I'm going to use an example of something that I saw in a little sidewalk café here in Victoria, British Columbia. There was a mom and her daughter, about 12 years old. They sat down to have lunch, and I could tell the girl was just pumped to have lunch with her mom. Just before the food came though, the mom's cell phone rang and she answered it. What I noticed most was the expression on the girl's face, who clearly knew what was going to happen. Because she ate her lunch by herself and her mom sat across the table that whole lunchtime talking on the phone. And the mom lost a chance to connect with her kid, contact that she's never going to get back."

Belonging is a critical element of learning, Martin believes. "I was once asked what are some of the key themes I saw in the last 30 or 40 years, and one of the central ones is that people who work with kids, especially educators, are moving to look at the whole child, whereas in the 1960s and 70s we were looking only at the cognitive aspect of the child. Now people are saying, wait a minute, if we want the kid to do well in math we also have to pay attention and tend to their emotional world, so we are looking at the child as a whole human being. And that's a good thing."

Try This!

Build a Culture of Belonging

What is your school's story? Your community's? To help create a culture of belonging, explore your school's or your community's history. What was there before it was built? How old is the school or community? Who were some of its former students or residents? If possible, you may want to look up some of the former students and residents and invite them to share their recollections, photos, and memorabilia with the students. Did the school or community ever undergo hardships? A flood, harsh winter, a fire? Or good times, such as a successful charitable event, a common goal, or a winning team? In what ways did the school or community come together to overcome or celebrate these events?

Ask the students what it means to be part of a community. Are people more likely to share their ideas when they feel they belong? How can we involve and tap into the unique talents of each person by helping them feel that sense of belonging? Try to implement some of the ideas the students come up with.

4 Lead the Way

Leadership Development

"If your actions inspire others to dream more, learn more, do more, and become more, you are a leader."

—John Quincy Adams

Before we explore the four primary conditions that support the imperatives described in Chapter 3, I'd like to take a moment to briefly outline the Lead the Way to Creativity initiative undertaken by the Ottawa-Carleton District School Board (OCDSB). My reason for doing so is that OCDSB has been recognized as a leader for its journey to creativity, and whether your organization is involved in education or not, this chapter provides a rough template you may want to follow or adapt for your own initiative. In addition, having an understanding of how Lead the Way took shape and its impacts can provide you with a deeper understanding of how the three imperatives and four conditions work together and build upon each other.

It all started one day in 2005, when the then–director of education Lorne Rachlis called me into his office and said, "I want you to take the lead for the district's leadership development portfolio." This took me by surprise. And he noticed.

As I mentioned, I was a guy who, at the age of 16, was encouraged by his teacher to quit school and get a job. To go from that view of myself to being asked to take responsibility for leadership development for a large school district of close to 80,000 students was indeed a shock. I tried to grasp the reasons he would want me for the job.

"I'm a bit of a different thinker," I began. "Perhaps you're looking for some changes?"

"Right then. Off you go." Lorne was a man of few words, but I had always respected his brilliant mind. He knew he was giving me an enormous opportunity, and I was extremely grateful.

The first thing I did was phone a guy who worked for the district named Frank Wiley. I didn't know Frank very well, but I had heard him talk on a few occasions and really appreciated his ideas. So I explained to him the opportunity that had come my way and asked if he'd be interested in getting together to think things through a little. Like where do you start when asked to take over the leadership development portfolio of a huge organization?

Frank agreed. We knew one of the first priorities would be to start a dialogue throughout the school district about our culture, people's perspectives on learning, and how we could move forward in a positive way. Beyond that, we didn't know what the hell we were doing.

Fortunately, hindsight comes with clarity, and looking back, we can now organize, categorize, and analyze the things we did, even though at the time it was more of an exercise in trial and error. We tried various things and took some risks; some worked very well and some didn't.

The reason I'm telling you this is that I am proud to be the kind of person that so many others can point to and say, "I learned from his mistakes." I hope that by describing the process here, and its successes, you may gain some insight on what your own quest to creativity might be like. It won't be as nice and neat as this guide appears, but when you hit roadblocks and make mistakes in your own transformational culture shifts, don't get discouraged and don't give up. Keep going!

While I was in the primary position for the leadership development portfolio, the journey itself, or the Odyssey as we came to think of it, proceeded in complex, weaving, and sometimes chaotic ways. The journey was only made possible because of the brilliance of the thousands of people who engaged, who thought, who pushed, who unselfishly contributed, sometimes into the night and the early morning hours, far beyond the call of duty. Custodians who read poetry at celebratory events, community members who spent hours constructing train sets to spark the fascination of young minds, dancers who perfected their routines to show us their understanding of the world, and tiny knitters who held us spellbound as they sat at a Lead the Way conference engaged in quiet conversation and knitting practical items for the less fortunate.

Lead the Way was a journey of complexity, and not unlike the words of my dear friend Bobby Moore, whom I mentioned in Chapter 1, it was not a matter of following a line into the future but of following many lines, some old and some new, and weaving them together to form a new future.

NINE YEARS OF LEARNING, DIVIDED INTO SEVEN NEAT STAGES

Looking back, I can see now that things were roughly divided into seven stages as we worked toward a culture that embraces creativity as a critical underpinning of our school board and the broader community.

Creating a Culture of Creativity

1. *The Spark*. An epiphany that emerged from one of the first meetings and the realization that we needed to hear from the people in the district about their reality of leadership and learning.

2. *The Study*. The process of the study we developed and conducted to hear from people across the district.

3. *The Findings*. What the study revealed to us.

4. *Next Steps*. The plans that grew out of the findings and served to create foundational structures on which to shift the district culture.

5. *Lead the Way Campaign*. The brand that became the vehicle to foster individual and organizational creativity.

6. *Creativity Demystified and Defined*. Keeping the momentum going to embed informal leadership as the soul of the district through the Lead the Way philosophy and events.

7. *Figuring Out the Specific Conditions to Foster Creativity in Our Organization*. There are at least four primary conditions to support the three imperatives described in the last chapter. However, every organization is different, with its own goals, culture, people, challenges, and opportunities. The conditions offered in *The Wonder Wall* are a great place to start, but you will also need to figure out whether there are other conditions specific to your organization. The best way to do this is to ask your employees, students, clients, and community what they think.

Stage #1: The Spark

Because we hadn't a clue what we were doing, Frank and I agreed we would start off by inviting 24 people, individuals from all of our employee groups, to a meeting to hear their views and ideas. We had superintendents sitting next to teachers, administrative assistants, custodians, and librarians—a diverse range of our workforce.

We wanted to provoke thinking, and so we distributed three articles for them to read: one on shared and distributed leadership, one on emotional intelligence in leadership, and a third about Margaret Wheatley's principles of community.

We divided the participants into three groups to read independently one of the articles and then share the learning and perspectives that emerged with the broader group so everyone could gain insight into the three topics.

Once that exercise was complete, we posed the question, "What does leadership mean to you?"

I would love to tell you that this led to an invigorating and perceptive exchange of ideas, but for the next hour, Frank and I listened to the crickets chirp and struggled along, trying to fill the deafening silence and coax reluctant responses from the group until, mercifully for us all, the meeting was drawing to a close.

And then something remarkable happened.

A gentleman sitting toward the back of the room, a man named Mike, put up his hand and said, "Can I ask a question?"

Given the rather bleak outcome of the entire meeting, I assumed the question would be a hostile one. Making an ill attempt at humor, I responded to his request with, "No, you cannot."

Fortunately for the future of the entire Lead the Way campaign, Mike ignored me and asked his question anyway. He said, "Why am I here?"

"Excuse me?" I replied. It wasn't exactly the question I'd been expecting.

"Why am I here?" he repeated, gesturing around the room. "Why was I invited to this meeting?"

I sputtered, still not understanding what he meant. I explained we were trying to gain as many diverse perspectives on leadership as possible so we could gain a baseline understanding of what it meant in our district. Any directions we developed regarding leadership had to be meaningful for everyone: We needed to be fundamentally inclusive in order to foster a culture of belonging, one that would really spark everyone's learning and engagement.

Now it was Mike's turn to be surprised. He responded that in all his years of working, he had never had the impression that his perspectives on matters such as these were relevant.

In retrospect, Frank and I realized that including employees from all groups and soliciting their ideas—something that rarely happens in any large organization—created a sense of uncertainty and unease among the participants. No one really knew what to make of the meeting or what was expected of them—or whether it was really safe to voice their honest opinions.

Thanks to Mike's courage in asking his question, however, the Lead the Way campaign received the spark it needed, and a lively first discussion was finally ignited that day.

It's important to note that Mike was a chief custodian. So this was not only a bold thing for him to do, but he had the courage to do it in front of people who were, in terms of positional authority, several steps up the district ladder. I'm not sure Mike recognized then that at our first discussion about leadership, he exemplified the very qualities of what true leadership means. His actions solidified my belief that we must flatten our hierarchies and understand the need to tap into the ideas and creative brilliance of every member of an organization if we, as a whole, are to achieve remarkable things and thrive.

Stage #2: The Study

After an initial series of small subgroup meetings, we decided to engage the district in the same type of process, because the purpose of the initiative was to foster leadership at all levels of the school community. So we designed a study that would engage the whole community in a discussion of leadership, which focused on three questions:

1. If you could create the ideal leader, what characteristics would the leader have?

2. How would the leader behave?

3. What are the consequences of being around a leader?

A second series of questions explored current practices of leadership among the school community:

1. What do you do that provides leadership?

2. Tell us about your leadership training in the school board. How does this help or hinder you?

3. Some people are leaders within their sites but do not want to be formal leaders. How can we help you as an informal leader?

This emphasis on the critical importance of informal leadership in fostering a healthy culture of belonging was very important to the conversation. We wanted people to understand that for us, the term *leadership* was not just about positional authority. Leadership pertains to the amazing things people do in their everyday lives and jobs that make positive impacts on those around them. We wanted to understand the behaviors and actions that contribute in an ongoing way to fostering a culture in which people feel welcomed and that they belong. In the context of a school district, where we are dealing with children in classrooms, this concept of informal leadership is pivotal.

Finally, the study asked respondents to share any other ideas they had about leadership in the school district.

Stage #3: The Findings

The results of the study were quite fascinating and gave us much to think about. First, there was significant agreement across all the employee groups about the perspective of characteristics, behaviors, and consequences of ideal leadership. Moreover, the study participants connected leadership consequences to "better results for staff and students" (Ottawa-Carleton District School Board, 2006).

This level of agreement across groups was, in the words of the study researchers, considered unusual.

This study also directed us on how we could start building on leadership best practices. The participant groups told us they would like to see the district:

- be inclusive in the practice of leadership;
- recognize leadership as enabling others;
- understand that leadership is a practice, not a title;
- recognize informal leadership; and
- provide opportunities to participate in leadership activities, including vision setting and decision making.

Ideal Leadership Characteristics

Ideal leadership characteristics differed little across the groups. They included the following:

- Good listener, approachable, personable
- Understanding, empathetic, respectful, caring
- Motivational, inspirational, visionary
- Honest, trustworthy, dependable, consistent
- Knowledgeable, informed, displaying expertise

- Good communicator
- Positive, enthusiastic, energetic

Interestingly, traditional management characteristics such as decisive/problem solver and organized/time manager were mentioned with much less frequency. Also, whereas *visionary* and *inspirational* were considered important qualities in a leader, they were not as important as characteristics that involve responsiveness to others, such as *empathetic, understanding, open,* and *supportive.* The consensus appeared to be that leadership is most importantly about enabling others.

HOW WOULD THE IDEAL LEADER BEHAVE?

Responses again showed striking similarity across employee groups. The ideal leader is accessible, supportive of those around him or her, and able to motivate others. He or she seeks input in an inclusive decision-making process. For instance, the desired behaviors of *lead by example* and *provide guidance and support* were mentioned twice as often as *take charge* and *decisive.* The most-mentioned ideal leader behaviors were the following:

- Leads by example
- Provides support, encouragement, motivation
- Seeks input
- Inclusive/fair
- Approachable/friendly
- Professional/responsible
- Positive/energetic
- Respectful
- Empathetic/understanding
- Team player/builds relationships

WHAT ARE THE CONSEQUENCES OF BEING AROUND A LEADER?

Again, responses were similar across employee groups. Consequences included personal benefits of feeling inspired and valued, professional benefits of learning and becoming a leader, team benefits in uniting colleagues and providing a shared vision, and school district benefits for students as the school community becomes more productive and creative.

Around an ideal leader, the work environment is supportive and collaborative and individuals and teams thrive. Consequences that received the most mentions included the following:

- Energized/inspired/brought out the best in people
- Good learning environment/became a leader/personal development/ learned through example
- Positive work environment/good morale
- Unites team/collaboration
- Supported/valued/confident
- Productive

Stage #4: Next Steps

This next stage was simple enough that we could take our cue from any 12-month-old: Once you've taken your first steps, don't sit on your butt; you have to take your next steps if you're going to get anywhere. Frank and I realized it was very important for us to establish credibility and trust by taking our next steps immediately after the study. This would send a strong message to our people in the district that we were serious, we had heard their voices, we were listening carefully, and we were dedicated to leadership practices that would capture their ideals.

EARN TRUST BY PUTTING IT IN WRITING

A Leadership Narrative

First, we decided to create a statement that captured the understanding of ideal leadership that had been so clearly articulated across all the groups in the district. We went back into the raw data, identified the most common resonant themes, and read the ideas and beliefs that people had so honestly and generously shared to create a leadership narrative.

Once we had all the themes and ideas mapped out, we thought the process of writing the leadership narrative itself would be relatively simple. We gathered together a diverse group of people, put ourselves in a room with a lot of coffee, and engaged.

The reality of creating the leadership narrative was hard work, however. A lot of hard work. There was a lot of pressure, because we knew every word counted, and every word would matter. It had to reflect what we had heard and serve as the foundational narrative for our pathway forward.

Once it had been crafted, however, our narrative immediately served as our leadership anchor and has continued to be so for more than a decade.

Leadership is exemplified by people who are able to impact those around them in a positive way. Our leaders are energetic, empathetic, motivated, trustworthy, knowledgeable, and good communicators. Our leaders share a common vision in their commitment to all students. Our leaders understand that their role is one of support. They lead by example, they seek input, and they listen. As an organization, we encourage and foster these qualities. In challenging and prosperous times, we are defined by the relationships we build.

Principles of Creative Leadership and Learning

Next, we recognized that those who had shared their ideas about leadership had given us an immense gift—the understanding that leadership is not a rank but (when given the chance) something that can flourish at every level of an organization. This clearly illustrated the first imperative for creative organizations described in Chapter 3, that everyone has a seed of brilliance within them.

Naturally, then, one of the most critical priorities in any organization is to figure out a way to unleash the potential that lies within every individual in its sphere of influence. This is particularly important in educational organizations. The more success we have in harnessing the unique capacities of every individual involved with students, the more likely we will be able to reach and teach every child in our care—who will then go out into the greater community and pass these gifts along.

The importance of the symbiotic connection between schools and the greater community can't be understated. In order to bring out the unique potential of each student, we have to look at individuals in a context that goes beyond the microcosm of the classroom or even the district.

Like a modern-day manifestation of the idea that it takes a village to raise a child, children eventually grow up to form the village. We must foster conditions that encourage leadership and creativity across all employee groups and then reach out into the community to engage partners from all areas: trades, business, nonprofits, health care, arts, sciences, and countless others. In this age of complexity, it is even more essential to tap into all the resources available. The responsibility for student learning is broad-based, and it's unfair to expect teachers to shoulder the burden alone. It also short-changes us. Every member of the community has something to offer, from which we will benefit in the long run through better and more innovative problem solvers, businesses, communities, and governments. When everyone in the community is engaged to that end, the job of teaching students becomes not only much more attainable but also more engaging, enjoyable, and inspirational. Enthusiasm is contagious; learning become celebratory.

With this in mind, we created our principles of creative leadership and learning, to set out in writing the need for inclusivity and to recognize the seed of brilliance in everyone.

- Each individual has unique creative capacities and ideas that need to be recognized, valued, and tapped into.
- By harnessing these individual capacities, the organization will be enriched and invigorated.
- The culminating effect will be to achieve a culture of engagement in which people feel valued and engaged in an environment that embraces ongoing learning fostered through internal and external dialogue and learning.
- This learning context will provide the optimal conditions in which we can reach and teach all the children within our care, enabling them to become successful global, digital citizens with strong creative and critical-thinking skills and an appreciation for diversity.

Stage #5: Lead the Way Campaign

In addition to our leadership narrative and principles of creative leadership and learning, we realized we needed a vehicle that would help embed these ideas throughout the mind-set of our various departments, schools, and classrooms. We created a brand called Lead the Way, which was designed to spread the idea that leadership and creative abilities exist within every one of us, as well as provide a way to share ideas and best practices.

The concept behind Lead the Way was that, whereas formal leadership is critical to the success of the organization, informal leadership—the wonderful things that people do in their everyday jobs, irrespective of their position—is equally critical. In a sense, informal leaders are the heart and soul of an organization. It was our intent that when people heard there was a Lead the Way event, they would instantly know it was open to anyone in or connected to the school community, regardless of job title or position.

Each year at the OCDSB, we had six to eight Lead the Way events that served a variety of purposes. They are always focused on the findings of the original leadership study, with a primary goal to grow the idea that leadership exists at all levels, in each individual, and that it is a practice, not a title. I'll discuss some of these events in more detail in our chapter about the condition of celebrating.

Lead the Way—Creative Initiatives

In addition, because creativity is often ingrained in people's minds as being confined to the arts, we used the Lead the Way events to put out calls for creative examples across all sectors and realms to our schools, the school district departments, the community, and everyone we could possibly find. This helped us to showcase how we benefited from the creative capacities of every person, helping us all to reach our full potential.

Stage #6: Creativity Demystified and Defined

If you want people to talk about the concept of creativity, then it is important that some common definition and understanding is agreed upon.

At this point, you might be wondering if our journey has veered off topic. I started this story talking about leadership, and now we're talking about helping to foster creativity. What does one have to do with the other?

Experts believe that to foster creativity, leadership and environments conducive to creativity are both necessary. Unless there is effective leadership at all levels, and unless people understand their unique capabilities and their ideas are valued, people rarely become engaged and passionate about what they are doing. Without engagement and passion, creativity cannot be cultivated, and informal leadership is unlikely to emerge.

To figure out what those conditions were, we began by consulting and collaborating with several renowned experts about the qualities of effective leadership and how to foster a creative environment, particularly in schools.

In the first few years of our Lead the Way initiative, we looked at creativity through multiple lenses. We brought in external experts who shared their understandings about these topics. We put these experts on the stage along with students who shared their own perspectives through forums, panels, and presentations, often expanding and building on the expertise of our guests. We also brought in community leaders, both formal and informal, from businesses, nonprofits, community organizations, and more, for discussions. At each gathering, we continued our quest to better understand the many questions we had:

What is imagination?

What is creativity?

What does imagination look like?

Why does it matter in the learning process?

Why do some people believe they are creative and others do not?

How do imagination and creativity connect with innovation? And entrepreneurship?

The wealth of diverse answers, ideas, recommendations, insight, and perspectives we gained allowed us to rethink exactly what creativity was. Ultimately, we wanted to settle on a definition of creativity that would serve our needs and help us understand what it would look like in our unique educational setting, in the classroom and across all departments of the district. Originally, we settled on three characteristics that defined creativity as something that

1. is original, new, or innovative;

2. has value or the capacity for effectiveness; and

3. is or can be practically implemented or created.

It was a good working definition, and it was similar to many other definitions we had come across in our research and discussions with creativity enthusiasts. But there seemed to be something missing.

One of the common criteria we had seen in other creativity definitions was the idea that creativity is a generator of solutions to *problems*. This aspect led to much discussion within our various groups and teams.

On one hand, the idea that creativity could only be invoked as a tool to generate some end-goal solution to a problem seemed to put rigid restrictions on what was supposed to be, after all, a process to promote free and unfettered thinking.

On the other hand, we could understand that creativity simply for the sake of creativity—an unbridled flow of disconnected ideas with no rigor, parameters, or goals in mind—might be fun to do with a few beers on a Saturday night but seemed to serve no practical purpose.

On this second point, we were also keenly aware that one of the main reasons countless organizations shy away from the idea of implementing creativity into their environments is that they view it as something nebulous, unproductive, and unmeasurable; the opposite of the lean processing and standardized procedures that have been ingrained into our organizational models over the past few decades.

As we grappled with these two key points of creativity that seemed to be at odds with each other, we found the answer was hiding right under our noses. As we rolled out our leadership narrative and guiding principles, we saw once again how a leader was not necessarily defined as a person with the ability to solve problems but as one with the ability to *bring out the best in others*.

Similarly, as we listened to our students, teachers, employees, and community guests at our Lead the Way events, we heard how they used creativity not just to solve problems but also to shine a light on "what could be" through transformation and change.

With this insight, the OCDSB added a fourth criterion to its definition of creativity, one that we have not seen included before:

4. Creativity can be used to solve problems or to apply strength-based techniques to catalyze positive transformation and change.

Stage #7: Figuring Out the Specific Conditions to Foster Creativity in Our Organization

By 2010, we'd spent several years engaging our school community in a process of defining creativity and in fostering the imaginative and creative capacities of every individual. We then decided to conduct an investigation into the conditions under which these processes would most likely occur. Our guiding research question was *What are the conditions under which creative and healthy individuals and organizations flourish?*

In tandem, we invited thousands of Lead the Way participants to share their own ideas about what conditions would help foster creative environments at the OCDSB and most crucially benefit the learning of students.

After we had documented several conditions, we realized that some were more pertinent to our unique needs. These needs were not only unique because we were a school board but also because of the particular demographic makeup of our population and opportunities the region offered us. For example, the city of Ottawa has the highest Inuit population outside of Canada's North. The capital region also straddles two provinces, Ontario and Quebec, and has a number of creative industries and a robust high-tech sector called "Silicon Valley North." We realized our most beneficial conditions might be somewhat different than those required for a business, or even by another school board, which would be located in a different set of circumstances.

Once we determined the conditions for our district, our entire journey was captured in a document called "Unleashing Potential, Harnessing Possibility: An Odyssey of Imagination, Creativity, and Critical Thinking. An Action Research Project of the Ottawa-Carleton District School Board." This document was extremely well-received, and to our delight, school boards and other organizations began to express an interest in what we were up to and asked if we could share what we learned about leadership, imagination, creativity, and innovation. If you'd like to read the report, it's available online at www.ocdsb.ca/ab-ocdsb/LeadTheWay/li/Pages/UnleashingPotentialharnessing Possibilities.aspx.

┌─ Try This! ─────────────────────────────

Let Your Students Lead Your
Next Leadership Development Event

The success of the Lead the Way campaign depended on many factors. Two of the most important, however, often have the hardest time gaining acceptance in a school or traditional business setting: recognizing that leadership exists at all levels and allowing people to take a risk. (Some of the best Lead the Way experiences and lessons learned came from taking risks!)

To get past this fear, why not try diving right in? The next time your school district has a leadership development session, why not let your students help plan it? Doing so would recognize and help develop your students' leadership skills and, although a bit of a risk, would certainly result in new and interesting ideas for your leadership development.

Start by asking students what kinds of new things they would like to learn or how we can make our classrooms more creative. What kinds of knowledge or skills do they think teachers would need to develop? How could they learn this? Are there experts in the community who could come in and do a workshop? Give the students a budget and let them organize the rest of the event as well, including lunch, presentations, a schedule, and maybe something completely different that you've never seen before. Include a group of students at the event and let them present their findings. Giving your students a voice such as this will certainly provide some interesting insights into how we can make our classrooms more creative!

5 Condition #1: Storytelling and Listening

*"A classroom lecture teaches the mind,
but a story teaches the heart."*

—Dr. Martin Brokenleg

In November 2010, Brandon Stanton, an unemployed history major who was scraping by on unemployment checks and loans from family and friends, started an online blogging project with a goal to capture the portraits of 10,000 ordinary people living in New York City. Interestingly, although his Humans of New York (HONY) project is now world famous, the growing collection of portraits was initially slow to gain a following.

That all changed when Stanton began talking to his subjects and posting their stories online along with their portraits. Within months, the popularity of the blog exploded. When Stanton's first HONY book was published in October 2013, it instantly became a bestseller. But some readers were disappointed the book didn't include the stories followers had come to expect with the online blog. Two years later, in October 2015, Stanton satisfied his followers' hunger to know the secrets, fears, and hopes behind the faces in the photographs, with the release of his *Humans of New York: Stories* book.

By June 2016, the Humans of New York Facebook page had almost 18 million likes, its Instagram account had more than 4.2 million followers, and Stanton had more than 300,000 followers on Twitter.

What I find interesting about Stanton's project is how his followers were fascinated to learn about the stories of ordinary people—people they had never met and were never likely to meet.

I believe there are a number of lessons we can learn from this, and these reveal why storytelling and listening are critical conditions that must be embedded in a classroom or an organization to foster creativity. Great teachers, like great business and community leaders, are almost always gifted storytellers.

As a reminder, here are the four conditions that foster creativity:

1. Storytelling and listening

2. Moving beyond diversity to inclusivity

3. Making it personal

4. Celebrating

WE ARE HARDWIRED TO LEARN FROM STORYTELLING

Learning through the written word is a relatively recent phenomenon in humankind's history. Although our ancestors are believed to have developed language some 100,000 years ago, written language didn't appear until about 95,000 years later. Moreover, even with the invention of Gutenberg's press in the 1400s, books and literacy did not become truly commonplace in Europe until the late 19th century, and later still in some other parts of the world.

That means that for the vast majority of our existence, we learned not from books but from each other. We learned through the tradition of storytelling—and very likely those stories derived from teachable moments and personal experiences. ("You want to poke that beehive with a stick? Let me tell you a story about what happened to your Uncle Nugg when he tried that.")

Storytelling is how we evolved, and in fact, research shows our brains are hardwired to listen and learn from storytelling.

Here's a simplified explanation of how it works. If you could look inside students' brains (as we've all been tempted to do), you would see two regions called Broca's area and Wernicke's area. Both spend their days processing language. When students read or hear words that are simply passing along information or are instructional in nature, such as an explanation of how to solve the Pythagorean theorem, the Broca and Wernicke areas (assuming the students are listening) will light up and display activity as they decode the words into meaning (Paul, 2012).

All well and good, but here's the really interesting part. If you conduct a brain scan on students (as we've all been tempted to do) while they are listening to or reading a story, whether fact or fiction, additional parts of the brain will also light up, especially those parts of the brain that correspond to the emotions, sensations, and feelings described. So if the story involves descriptions of the cinnamon scent of a freshly baked apple pie cooling on the windowsill, the aroma of fresh-cut grass, the syncopated rhythms of a big jazz band, the burning red embers of a summer campfire, or a lost kitten mewling in the rain, the areas of the brain responsible for processing those senses and emotions become activated—as yours just did while reading these descriptions. Likewise, if the story describes someone briskly running down a path, jumping into a cold lake, or falling out of bed, the students' motor cortex, responsible for movement, also springs to life.

Keith Oatley, professor emeritus of cognitive psychology at the University of Toronto, as well as a novelist, has done much research on the subject. He likens storytelling to reality simulations that "run(s) on minds of readers just as computer simulations run on computers." These simulations not only make for more exciting and engaging learning opportunities, they allow people to experience the thoughts and feelings of others—to get right inside their heads—without actually having lived the experience. It literally allows us to build experiences and have a "social dress rehearsal" in a safe environment before experiencing the real thing.

In fact, Dr. Raymond Mar, a psychologist at Canada's York University, who has worked with Dr. Oatley, found our brain networks that are used to understand stories overlap with our networks used to navigate interactions with others, such as trying to figure out what others are thinking or feeling, or their motives. In other words, listening to or reading stories hones our real-life social skills. In two other studies collaborated by Drs. Oatley and Mar and other scientists, it was found that individuals who frequently read fiction seem to better understand other people and to be able to empathize with them. Another study by Dr. Mar found the same was true even in preschool-age children.

Researcher Uri Hasson, from Princeton University, found that when a person is telling a story, his or her brain and the brains of listeners will actually synchronize. In his TED Talk "This Is Your Brain on Communication," he describes how the brain region activity of volunteer listeners closely followed and matched the activity of the storyteller's brain regions.

It's therefore easy to see why students and all people become more engaged in the subject at hand if it is relayed through storytelling. It's because they literally *are* more engaged: More areas of their brain are actively involved in not simply decoding the instructional message but actually *living* it.

STORYTELLING HELPS US TO CREATE CULTURES OF BELONGING, ONE OF THE THREE IMPERATIVES FOR CREATIVITY

Stories bind us together as a community in at least three important ways. One is our shared stories, or shared history, legends, and lore. Knowing where we came from, the challenges and joys our people experienced, and our traditions and customs and how they began weaves a rich tapestry that binds us together. Moreover, it helps us understand where we, as individuals, fit into the pattern—how the threads of our lives weave into the tapestry and make it both stronger and more colorful.

The second important way that storytelling helps to create cultures of belonging is by sharing our own personal stories with each other. By knowing more about who each of us is, we begin to understand each other. Knowing the personal story behind the children in our classrooms, the people we work with, and the people in the broader community helps us to empathize with them, as well as helps us to uncover the talents, insights, and knowledge that we otherwise would not know they possess.

Finally, a third aspect of storytelling helps each of us to personally feel we fit in. It's comforting to know that we're not alone in our thoughts, feelings, and situations; by hearing others' stories, we realize that others have traveled or are traveling down the same path we are. Moreover, reading or hearing about others' experiences or aspirations similar to our own helps us to practice our social, communication, and coping skills—because, as noted, stories activate parts of the brain that help us to experience what situations are like.

Now, to understand why a culture of belonging is such an essential condition for storytelling and ultimately for creativity to take place, you need only to think back to those times that you felt like you weren't sure you *did* belong, or at least not yet. That first day in a new town or that first day you walked into the high school cafeteria. That first day at a new job and those times you sat around a boardroom table, wondering if the others present knew what an imposter you were.

When you think about those times, how likely were you to raise your hand or venture to speak, let alone share your ideas, especially the more unusual ones? Or heaven forbid, how often did you dare to share an opinion that didn't agree with or support the opinions of the leaders around the table?

Unless people feel that they belong, and are safe, and that their ideas, insights, and contributions are welcome and valued, then they will not share them. It's as simple as that.

WE NEED STORYTELLING TO DEVELOP EMPATHY, ANOTHER VITAL FACTOR FOR CREATIVITY

In 2010, a study from the University of Michigan revealed a shocking statistic: Empathy among college students had dropped a whopping 40 percent compared to their counterparts who attended college in the 1980s and 90s— and the biggest drop occurred in the 10-year period from 2000 to 2010 (Swanbrow, 2010).

The research, which analyzed data from 72 studies on empathy and involved 14,000 American college students from 1979 to 2009, found that today's students were less likely to agree with statements such as the following:

- I sometimes try to understand my friends better by imagining how things look from their perspectives.
- I often have tender, concerned feelings for people less fortunate than me.
- I believe there are two sides to every question and try to look at them both.

There are many wide-ranging theories about why this sudden drop in empathy has occurred, and certainly much more research needs to be done before any hard conclusions can be drawn. I'm no expert, but I'm quite certain that there is far more than one factor involved. For the purposes of this book, I'd like to offer some personal insights about how empathy relates to storytelling, education, diversity and inclusivity (which we'll discuss as a condition in the next chapter), creativity, and ultimately, to students' learning experiences in our classrooms.

First, as we all know, there have been massive changes in our world since 1979, and I believe this has led to a state of complexity. During times of complexity, there is a great deal of uncertainty and anxiety. Moreover, some of these changes have had a particularly direct and profound impact on younger generations and families.

WE NEED TO BRING BACK FREE PLAY

Families increasingly need a dual income in our society, resulting in the rise of afterschool programs, day care, organized activities, and summer camps— all on top of spending time in the classroom. The challenge here is that we have come to define "quality" education and "quality" childcare (sometimes even "quality" time with parents) as having certain attributes that, like standardized tests, might too narrowly define what we should be focused on.

In times of complexity, those who want to feel in control of globalization and the rapid pace of change feel a duty to heavily regulate and schedule children's and students' activities, usually with an objective for them to master a subject or sport, so they will succeed in what we perceive as a far more competitive world these days. We can see this even in the way many pre-schools are named, with "little learners" or "scholars" in the title. This focus on what we consider "productive time" leaves little to no time for free play.

(Interestingly, we can see the same philosophy and many parallels behind the "lean processing" practices used in today's businesses.)

To see what I mean, take a look at guidelines for "quality childcare." Upfront you will likely see regulations for minimum standards of health and safety, hygiene, building codes, and the like, followed by training, wages and working conditions, staff-child ratios and group sizes, and auspice, or who owns the facility. Then, even for toddlers, there will be guidelines for educational elements, which often include pedagogical approach, curriculum framework, an educational philosophy, and the variety of educational goals for children to achieve. Guidelines for fun and active play are often mentioned only later in such guidelines.

This is important because free play is how children naturally develop empathy. All interactive play needs to be defined by rules, or at least some kind of agreement on how the play will proceed, whether it's a game of kick the can or let's pretend we're dinosaurs. To negotiate these rules or agreements, children must listen to their peers, hear them out, weigh the pros and cons, state their opinions in a way that they will be heard and considered, and negotiate fairly—which requires putting themselves in the shoes of their peers and trying to see their point of view. The result is an organic growth of empathy.

With the structure and definition of quality care, however, children don't have opportunities to practice this skill as much as they should. Too often, adults decide which activity will happen next, the activity location, the parameters of the play, and the rules and consequences for those who don't comply. This isn't to say children don't need supervision and guidance, but children experience a very different kind of play than they did just 30 years ago.

It's a tough challenge, and finding solutions won't be easy. But it's something we need to look at, because in addition to challenges with empathy, it appears the decline in free play may also be leading to the increased depression and anxiety we are seeing among our children and youth.

Dr. Peter Gray (2011), who researches play through a biological-evolutionary perspective, says free play is essential for children's healthy social and emotional development, as it is for all mammals. In his recent TEDxNavesink presentation and in his article *The Decline of Free Play and the Rise of Psychopathology in Children and Youth*, Gray talks about how the decline of free play is occurring in lockstep with a dramatic increase in anxiety, depression, feelings of helplessness, suicide, and narcissism in children and youth. He also provides steps we can take to help bring free play back into the lives of our children.

THE RISE OF SOCIAL MEDIA

With the rise of social media, people have an opportunity to keep in contact with more people, in more ways, than ever before. In this context, one might think social media would promote more social interaction and connectedness, not only allowing people to share photos, videos, and opinions but also ideas, knowledge, and learning experiences.

Personally, I would argue that social media has the potential to create more empathy on a broader level, because it offers the opportunity to explore so many different and diverse points of view. They say that centuries ago, the vast majority of people spent their entire lives never traveling farther than three to five miles from their place of birth. Now we can view the lives of people living half a world away in an instant. Theoretically, this exposure to diversity should foster and develop empathy, allowing individuals to practice putting themselves into the shoes of others.

However, this is not how social media is playing out. For one thing, research shows that people under the age of 40 are using their cell phones to text more than talk. According to Neil Howe (2015), big businesses such as JPMorgan Chase, Coca-Cola, Bank of America, and Citigroup are getting rid of voice mail altogether, for their employees increasingly prefer to use texting, e-mail, and social media to communicate with clients. A 2014 Gallup poll, explained by Frank Newport in "The New Era of Communication Among Americans," confirms that all age groups increasingly prefer to text and e-mail rather than talk, and the younger you are, the more likely you are to follow this trend.

Over a mere two years, from 2008 to 2010, Nielsen data showed the average monthly voice minutes used by 18- to 34-year-olds plummeted by 25 percent, from 1,200 to 900 minutes per month, while texting grew 233 percent, from 600 to 1,400 per month (Newport, 2014).

What's behind this societal shift away from phone calls, especially among millennials? Some research suggests it's because they feel that reading tones, emotions, and body language just gets in the way. I would suggest there's also a perception of less social risk in communicating electronically. You can take the time to figure out exactly what you want to say and reword it several times if necessary, unlike a face-to-face or telephone conversation. And yes, many people prefer text because it helps them to avoid interacting with people.

E-mail and texting are being used to avoid voice and face-to-face communications. A study by the Pew Research Center showed that *more than half* of teenagers *preferred* communicating with friends through text and social media rather than face-to-face (Lenhart, 2015). And this is even more apparent when engaging in difficult conversations: According to a *USA Today* survey, six out of ten 21- to 50-year-olds would be okay breaking up with someone they were dating casually via text, and a quarter would even end a serious relationship this way (Jayson, 2013).

Ghosting, an even more recent trend, is the practice of ending romantic and platonic relationships with no communication at all—one simply stops responding to any texts, voice mails, and other attempts at communication until the dumped person gives up and goes away.

Scary, given our understanding of the critical importance of listening and storytelling to our learning, both individually and collectively.

I WANT IT AND I WANT IT NOW: THE INCREASING PREVALENCE OF INSTANT GRATIFICATION

Another societal change that does little to foster empathy is the increasing desire for instant gratification. Want proof? If an online video doesn't start up within five seconds, 25 percent of people will abandon it. By 10 seconds, more than half are gone, and by 20 seconds, 80 percent have left (Muther, 2013).

But developing empathy takes time, practice, experience, and sometimes hard work and effort, especially when a person is very different from us. When we are unable to connect with another individual easily and readily, or have to take the time and make the effort to read facial expressions and put ourselves in another's shoes, it's tempting to simply move on.

Dr. Martin Brokenleg, whom I mentioned earlier, told us how he believes storytelling is a type of learning that is critical to teaching empathy and other skills.

"We tend to teach a person's mind through lectures, and that is important because people need factual information," says Dr. Brokenleg. "But when we look at the dynamics that make it possible for a person to live, that's a different type of learning. It tends to be experiential and we poetically talk about it as learning something in the heart. Having been a therapist for 40 years, I can tell you it is heart learning that really matters in a person's life."

He adds that, "A classroom lecture teaches the mind, but a story teaches the heart. The important themes that give a person stability in life are heart learnings."

HOW IS STORYTELLING AND LISTENING CONNECTED TO CREATIVITY?

Storytelling is an essential condition to fostering creativity for a number of reasons, but many of the changes we're experiencing in this time of complexity, such as more scheduled structure, less free play, a preference for faceless communication, and a desire for instant gratification, actively work against supporting the art of storytelling and active listening skills.

Before I go any further, I would like to point out that I'm not criticizing these changes that have occurred. Changes such as dual-income families, increasing technology, and faster services have also brought immense social benefits, and besides, these horses are so far out of the barn they're probably running in the Kentucky Derby by now.

But there are many things we can and must do to bring back the art of storytelling and active listening so that our classrooms, businesses, and society can reap their benefits and set the stage for creativity to flourish. As the overwhelming success of Stanton's Humans of New York project indicates, knowing other people's stories is something we crave.

We are hardwired to listen to stories, and I would argue we are also hardwired to create and tell stories. Human beings are consummate storytellers. The stories we tell reveal the essence of who we are: our interests, passions, strengths, fears, weaknesses, and aspirations. A key condition of learning is that we listen astutely and carefully to the people around us. The more we understand people and their stories, the more insight we have into their unique capacity.

There is a rather humorous study by Fritz Heider and Marianne Simmel that took place at Smith College in 1944 that perfectly captures our intrinsic need to tell stories. In it, 34 college students were shown a short film in which a circle and two triangles (one large and one small) moved around the screen and past a stationary rectangle. When asked what was happening in the film, only one student stated the obvious: It was a bunch of geometric shapes randomly moving around. All the other students came up with imaginative stories, which included not only such narratives as one of the triangles was out to get the others and a battle was ensuing but even assigning emotions to the geometric characters such as "worried" and "enraged."

LEARNING TO LISTEN

Some say that listening has become a lost art, but in our complex world, I think it's become more than that. It's increasingly common that people try to censor and silence opposing views, not allowing others to speak at all. In schools and other communities, this can be seen in zero tolerance policies and guest speakers being uninvited to events. At protests, opposing sides shout each other down or use white noise machines, attempting to drown out voices. On social media, people attempt to discredit opposing views, creating photoshopped memes to shame those who hold different views.

These tactics may begin with a noble intent to change society for the better, and let's face it, sometimes opinions can be downright hateful and extremely hurtful to the person or group they're directed at.

The problem with these tactics, however, is they don't work. I will guarantee you no one in the history of humankind has ever changed their opinion by being told to shut up or by being called stupid or worse. Silencing a person doesn't make his or her viewpoint go away or change it, it simply drives it underground, where it continues to fester and grow. It leaves the individual frustrated, angry, and alienated—a frame of mind that is even less conducive to learning a different point of view.

Once you take away a person's voice by refusing to listen to them, by refusing to allow them to share their story and why they feel the way they do, you have lost the opportunity to teach them—or enable them to teach you (perhaps it is your opinion that may change!). Zero tolerance means zero learning. Taking a strength-based approach, we need to see every hateful or negative statement on either side of the fence as a teachable moment, an opportunity to help bring out the best in others by helping them to achieve greater insight, have less fear, and become part of a greater community. It also helps us to learn more about unmet needs that may be causing a problem and address them. Learning is, after all, a two-way street meant to lead to solutions for the benefit of all.

If we really want to change society for the better then, especially in these times of complexity, we need to value stories as our ancestors did. Storytelling is how they passed down knowledge and wisdom from one generation to the next, but they also understood the connection between storytelling and personal and collective meaning. They understood that stories and humor make lasting bonds and provide deep spaces of belonging. Familiarity doesn't breed contempt; it breeds understanding and acceptance.

We need to put stories and listening back into the core of our classrooms, family, and work lives, to support the imperatives of developing spaces of belonging and the understanding that there is a seed of brilliance and leadership in everyone. When children don't find these spaces at home, in the classroom, or in the community, they turn to alternate groups to find that sense of belonging and develop other means of creating and sharing their own stories. When people don't have spaces for sharing, it creates an environment where loneliness and mental health issues can take root and grow.

In Stephen Haff's Still Waters in a Storm program, discussed in Chapter 3, he tells the children about the importance of listening. He tells the students that listening is a great gift to give another person: "Some people don't have a place where they can go, where someone will listen to them. I think a lot of people don't have that. Everyone needs a place where they can just sit and someone will listen to what they have to say. It's really important to have that. It's a great gift that you're giving to each other."

The stories read aloud at Still Waters are not always pretty. They don't all have happy endings. They sometimes talk about abuse, violence, drugs, loneliness, racism, and the harsh realities of living in a rough neighborhood, with families who are often just scraping by. But by sharing these stories, a community of belonging is built. One former student, who used to belong to a gang, now volunteers at Still Waters. He says that instead of giving him detention, Stephen used to give him books. Stories became a way of showing him a different world and a different path he could take. His views changed; had he simply been silenced, the chances for turning his life around certainly would have been much slimmer.

HOW TO EMBED STORYTELLING INTO YOUR CULTURE

The key for learning organizations is to find ways of revealing peoples' stories and to harness the uniqueness that lies within them. There are a number of ways to do this, and I think the best way to illustrate is to tell the story of Alexandra "Sacha" Hamilton, Duchess of Abercorn, and the Pushkin Trust.

When we spoke to her, she explained how her story began in 1986 in Ireland, during the time of social unrest sometimes referred to as the Troubles. Despite her mother trying to shield her from the news, Sacha's daughter, Sophie, was having nightmares about her home being invaded and the family being attacked. She wasn't alone.

Sacha says, "There was a toxin, a fear in the air that every child was feeling and breathing at that time. Sophie was very disturbed. And I couldn't really tell her, no, we won't be attacked because no one knew what was going to happen next. I didn't know how to reassure her."

Then one summer weekend, Sacha was invited to her grandmother's home in England for a commemoration of the life of her ancestor, Alexander Pushkin. Pushkin (1799–1837) is considered by many to be the greatest Russian poet of all time and the founder of modern Russian literature.

"Something extraordinary happened during those three days," says Sacha. "People from very diverse backgrounds came together, from Russia, from America, from France, England, Ireland, everywhere, and we were all singing from the same hymn sheet, all because of Pushkin.

"He was an artist of such universal voice, and it carried us into the realms of being human, whether it was in sorrow or joy, and that welded us together. It made new common ground for us."

It gave Sacha an idea. If Pushkin's writing could help draw diverse people together in England, could a common theme of writing literature help bring Catholic and Protestant schools together in Ireland? She envisioned giving children like her daughter Sophie a voice, an opportunity to write down their feelings and emotions and express themselves creatively.

Sacha took her idea to the education board, and the idea, or the Pushkin Trust as it came to be known, began to grow. It was decided that instead of simply connecting Catholic and Protestant students through writing in Northern Ireland, they would also approach the Republic of Ireland. "At the time, we had no connection with the Republic educationally," says Sacha. "In fact, we were more or less at war with each other."

Nevertheless, everyone was happy to get involved. Eight schools started off, with four from the south and four from the north. "They chose teachers who they felt would respond to this creative side of education, and these teachers jumped at the idea."

What surprised the teachers the most, however, was the impact on the students. Sacha explains, "In particular, it was the lowest academic achievers who were given a chance to find their voice and to write stories for their friends and peer groups. Those children were now becoming motivated not only to write stories but to improve their writing and their spelling. As more teachers heard about these results, the Pushkin Trust simply snowballed. I think the teachers really took to it because children normally write factual things, to get the answers right, and aren't often asked to write about their feelings. It brought the heart back into the classroom."

In the early days, the children were asked to tell their personal story, to write about themselves, where they came from, and what they were thinking about. In later years, the children were given themes related to earth, air, fire, and water, the four elements of life.

Sacha shares, "One year we would have a theme of the living tree, which is earth, and another we would have the river of life, which is water and flow, or the fire within, so the theme crosses the curriculum and touches every subject. For example, if you think about flow, it could encompass blood flow and biology. It can touch every subject the teacher wants to do."

Originally, Pushkin prizes were awarded for commendable writing, but after a number of years Sacha thought better of the practice. "We felt we shouldn't be judging children for their feelings and thoughts. We are trying to help a child grow to full potential, and that is the birthright of every child, to develop your head, your heart, your emotions, your instincts—the whole of yourself. Pushkin is about being able to express feelings creatively, and no longer destructively, which is what we were doing to ourselves in Ireland.

"Now the children assess themselves. They are getting their own sense of achievement and their own sense of improvement. They come to feel better about themselves by the end of it."

The Pushkin project also supports the voice of the teacher through its Inspiring Educator program, which provides an initiation for teachers into the work so that they in turn can release the voice of the child. "We strongly advocate not just professional development of a teacher but also personal development," says Sacha.

LESSONS LEARNED

What we can learn from Sacha and the Pushkin Trust can help us to embed a culture of storytelling into our schools and organizations.

- View storytelling and listening not as simply classroom exercises but as a long-term means to support the imperatives of creating cultures of belonging and recognizing a seed of brilliance in everyone.
- Don't always feel the need to grade or judge the stories. As we've seen, both Still Waters and the Pushkin Trust had better engagement with students when judging did not take place.
- Use storytelling across the curriculum.
- Ask your students to tell you their stories, and in return, tell them yours. Tell them about times when you have felt frightened, brave, happy, or lonely or witnessed something funny.
- Take your students to meet a diverse range of people and interview them about their stories—retirees, a police officer, a fire fighter, the principal, entrepreneurs—the world is rich with stories.
- Invite the community in to tell their stories. At the OCDSB, schools with high populations of new Canadians were invited to come in and share their stories of where they lived before and what it was like to move to Canada, creating empathy and supporting cultures of belonging.
- If you overhear your students making negative, racist, or sexist remarks, sit down and ask them how they came to hold those views. What are the feelings behind them? Could learning more about the source of fear change their views? What are more appropriate, less hurtful ways to express fear?

Stories From the Field

Following Dreams Through Self-Expression

Living in Colorado, Khadija Grant is an author of several novels, a blogger, a mother of three, and a keen advocate for fostering creativity in children and youth. She understands the connection between fostering storytelling—the ability to express one's thoughts, ideas, and emotions—and learning. In an unscripted and very moving video she posted, she describes the experience of what happens when storytelling and listening are not embedded in the environment. Here is a summary:

"I just left a high school, and I was supposed to talk about what I did and talk about the Harlem Renaissance. I started talking about how the Harlem Renaissance was amazing because people were able to express themselves. They knew how to express themselves, they knew what they liked because they had been oppressed for so long. [I told these students] how they and adults should express themselves, through writing, through self-expression, art, whatever they feel.

"But after I talked, the youth came up to me and started sharing their stories. And it is so sad and touching how, we as parents, we as a society, we keep these children in a box. Literally in a box, to a point that they don't even know who they are. They don't even know what they want out of life. I'm talking about juniors, 11th graders. It's just sad, because some of the kids were crying.

"I was asking them, what is your dream? Not your mom's dream, not your father's dream, but what is your dream? [And their answer is] 'I don't know.' Another person . . . [I asked him], 'What do you love?' 'I don't know.'

"When you are in 11th grade, and you don't know how to express yourself, that's oppression. That is oppression. In my eyes, that's sad. I don't know what we are doing for our children, but we are creating, literally, robots. People and children who cannot express themselves, who can't feel, who don't know how to feel . . .".

Khadija voices her concerns about raising children with only the goal of college in mind. "I want my children to know who they are and what they want, and I want them to go for it; I don't want them to wait, they can do it right now. Because that feeling of oppression drives people crazy."

To help get children thinking about their dreams, in 2016, Khadija authored the children's book *You Can Start One Too*, illustrated by

Kimberley Clark. In the story, a young girl visits various businesses in her community and learns how the owners and entrepreneurs followed their dreams.

"Who owns this place?" I ask.

"It's really, really cool!"

"I do, my friend," a woman says.

"And I started just like you.

I imagined it. I planned it.

I made my dreams come true.

And if you really like it,

You can start one, too."

What a wonderful message to send to children!

Grant, Khadija. *You Can Start One Too.* Illustrated by Kimberly Clark, Khadija Grant L.L.C., 2016

Try These!

Humans of Our Classroom

Take a page from the Humans of New York project and create a Humans of Our Classroom art and story gallery for the wall of your classroom. Share the Humans of New York project with your students, then help them learn the basics of photography, interviewing techniques and questions that provoke thoughtful answers (come up with a list as a class activity), and the art of listening. Then let them loose to create their own Humans of Our Classroom portraits and stories. For best results, don't pair children off to interview each other, but let each student draw a name from a hat, so students are not interviewing the same student who interviewed them. After the project, ask students what they learned about the person they interviewed that they never knew before. Were they surprised? Discuss if sharing stories changing things and why. If your school has enough teachers, you could alternatively pair off each student to interview a teacher.

Humans of Our Community

Take the Humans of Our Classroom project a step further and enable students to learn more about the people in their community through storytelling. To find willing participants, ask your local retirement home or seniors' center if they'd be willing to set aside an hour to enable each student to meet one-on-one with a senior or a staff member. Offer to share the stories and photographs with them.

Another possibility is to set up a similar arrangement with local shopkeepers or a farmer's market through their local business association, or the employees of a larger, locally owned business. Local cultural groups and associations may also be interested in sharing their stories. If you know any educators abroad, you could also arrange interviews between the two classrooms internationally. Or ask the students to interview and photograph a parent or family member.

Host a Living Library

Invite a variety of individuals from your community into your school library for an hour—either physically or virtually. Students can then "check out" these real-life human stories to ask questions and hear their histories and opinions.

Let Your Students Know You're Human

When it comes to storytelling, be a model for your students. Was there a subject in school you had a hard time understanding? How did you feel? What happened? Did you ever feel left out or excluded? What made a difference? And don't be afraid to bring in the human stories of the subject matter you're teaching, for storytelling can elicit the emotional response that helps students learn. Before launching into the Pythagorean theorem, it might help to explain Pythagoras was a real person, with a son and three daughters—one of whom married a famous wrestler of the time.

6

Condition #2: Moving Beyond Diversity to Inclusivity

"Today, when I think about diversity, I actually think about the word 'inclusion.' And I think this is a time of great inclusion. Whether it's geographic, it's approach, it's your style, it's your way to learning, the way you want to contribute, it's your age, it really is broad."

—Ginni Rometty, Chairwoman, President, and CEO of IBM

Whenever I speak about diversity being an essential condition for fostering creative organizations, I'm met with a confident response. "Oh, yes, diversity! We've already got a diversity plan in place for our organization, and it's working quite well."

If there's one essential condition for creativity that people invariably understand, and that common sense tells us is true, it's diversity. The more diverse a group is, the more diverse their ideas, knowledge, and expertise will be. In fact, the more I think about it, the more I realize creativity and diversity are synonymous.

However, the fostering of diversity in organizations is a very complex task, and some traditional methods have not resulted in the increased creativity expected.

The story of my friend Nellie (not her real name) helps to explain what I mean. During her 25-year career as a consultant, Nellie has sat around dozens of executive boardroom tables in the public, private, and academic sectors. She has worked with more than a hundred businesses, government departments, and academic organizations, often to help them communicate new leadership and change initiatives to employees, suppliers, and clients.

Nellie is old enough to remember the days when those sitting around the executive boardroom table were a fairly homogeneous group. But even in the early days of her career, there were increasing calls for more diversity in the workforce in general and around those top-floor boardroom tables in particular.

This was a welcome and exciting prospect for Nellie. She, too, understood the obvious: Having a greater diversity of people sitting around the boardroom table meant having a greater diversity of knowledge, experiences, and leadership capabilities from which to draw fresh, new ideas—it was the very foundation of creativity. And more creativity, she reasoned, should lead to more innovative, and therefore more successful, businesses, schools, and organizations.

Often, the strategy to bring more diversity to the boardroom included tactics to encourage hiring and promotions from certain targeted groups that weren't demographically well represented. Nellie sat back and waited for the groups she worked with to become more diverse and ultimately more creative.

The years went by. As faces around the boardroom tables came and went, Nellie observed that the strategy appeared to have mixed results. For some demographic groups, she saw little change; others were perhaps somewhat more successful. For women, fortunately, the strategy seemed to work quite well, at least in the places Nellie worked, and eventually there were as many women sitting around the table as men, sometimes even more, and it wasn't unusual for them to hold the CEO and senior leadership titles.

Nellie greatly admired these women. They were bold, smart, strategic, and not afraid to speak their minds. So although Nellie was disappointed that the diversity strategy hadn't had a stronger impact on bringing some other underrepresented groups to the table, she was very encouraged by seeing more females join the executive ranks and eager to see how much more innovative and creative these leadership teams would become with this added diversity.

But as more time passed, creativity within the top ranks was . . . well, less than expected. Nellie noticed that even though these diversity initiatives changed some of the voices at the table, everyone was still singing the same song. The ideas, viewpoints, approaches, leadership styles, processes, topics discussed, and types of solutions put forth showed only very modest changes, or virtually none at all. In particular, the transformational leadership and organizational culture programs, to be cascaded and communicated to employees, were essentially along the same top-down-driven motivational and change-management programs Nellie had encountered when she first started her career.

Now before we go a step further, I want to emphasize I am not in any way criticizing the policies and programs that strived to put more diversity into the workforce and into leadership roles. That movement was and still is essential and succeeded in removing some of the barriers for those who wanted and deserved a fair chance to climb the corporate ladder. For this book, we are only observing the perplexing result this diversity strategy had on creativity. Even with the modest increases in diversity that Nellie had witnessed, shouldn't she have seen at least some corresponding increases in new ideas and creativity?

The answer to this puzzle came to Nellie one day as an executive team was chatting among themselves while waiting for some technical difficulties to be resolved for a presentation. There was a new hire in the group, and they were all comparing notes about various aspects about where she had come from and where she could find various services and amenities in her new hometown.

Nellie describes it thus: "As they shared the details of their lives, it suddenly occurred to me just how much this group of people had in common. Out of curiosity, I started to do a little more digging into the backgrounds of this team and other executive teams (easy to do with LinkedIn, Facebook, and Google) to uncover the inner lives and workings of just what made a C-suite executive.

"What I found was that most had grown up in one of three major cities, and a lot even had lived in the same neighborhoods, vacationed in the same destinations, and even had friends in common, either from childhood, university, or from working earlier at other organizations in their careers.

"While not all of them came from wealthy families, nearly all had done well in school, getting not only excellent marks but also being student leaders who were involved in extracurricular activities. All but one had gone on to postsecondary school, many to the same top universities in Canada, the U.S., or Europe, and had taken the same degrees and programs. They had also attended many of the same executive development programs, particularly for MBAs.

"Most fell within a 10-year age span and were accordingly within a similar span for life stages, being married (or divorced) and even having children of about the same age attending the same schools, sports camps and activities, driving similar vehicles, and living in the same neighborhoods and types of dwellings.

"Perhaps the biggest common denominator for these executives, however, was their ambition and drive. It made sense, really—you couldn't reach that level or do the work required if you weren't driven to do that kind of thing. As such, every single one was a high-energy, competitive, self-confident, decision-oriented individual who actually thrived on putting in the long hours and effort it takes to make it to the very top."

While working at another company with another team on talent acquisition and succession planning, Nellie realized that the typical hierarchical organizational structure itself helps drive homogeneity and conformity on the top floor. She explains, "Just look at any job requirements or descriptions for an executive leadership position. They all basically require the same things—an advanced degree in a narrow number of fields, for which the prerequisite is academic excellence and leadership participation at the secondary level; a certain number of years of experience, which puts contenders in about the same age range by the time they reach the top; an expectation that the executive will work long hours, including travel, and put in significant effort and dedication to the organization, which requires ambition and drive; and a compensation package that puts those around the boardroom table in a similar financial bracket, enabling them to live and play in the same neighborhoods and vacation spots.

"In their talent management strategies, each executive team sought to replace retiring executives or attract new hires according to virtually the same educational path and years of experience as they had in the past," Nellie says. "In some cases, they simply pulled up the previous job posting, made a few adjustments, and reposted it."

Due to these factors, Nellie found that despite the diversity initiatives, the executive team members were very much alike on the inside. "It wasn't that the intentions hadn't been good, or that these executive teams weren't hardworking and sincere in their desire to be more diverse and creative. They absolutely were. But the odds for success were stacked against them, due to the typical organizational structure of executive leaders at the top coming up with ideas and making decisions and plans that governed the activities of the ranks below them. It acted as a filter to sift out all but a certain type of personality with a certain type of background—regardless of gender, ethnicity, or other physical characteristics."

And once at the boardroom table, groups tended to become even more homogenous, Nellie noted. "Now they were all working for the same company, with the same colleagues, in the same city, often on the same floor."

Later, when Nellie worked on a project with a small team to help promote more inclusion of a particular group that, in her experiences, had seen very little increase at the boardroom table, she discussed her observations with the team leader, a member of the demographic.

"He explained to me that my observations were not unusual," Nellie recalls. "It wasn't that members of the demographic were any less academically prepared or lacking in leadership capabilities, but the road to the boardroom table—office politics, striving to get ahead, being competitive, putting work ahead of social relationships or family—were not as relevant in their culture, which tended to value entrepreneurship and group collaboration over personal ambition. This concerned me because if this demographic wasn't as attracted to securing a seat at the boardroom table, at least in the way typical organizations and hierarchies are currently structured, how would their ideas be heard or their talents shared?"

Dr. Martin Brokenleg agrees that being aware of cultural differences can play an important role in promoting diversity and inclusivity and help us recognize the creative spark in others.

"I believe there is a very close connection between creativity and diversity. If you foster diversity, you will find creativity," Dr. Brokenleg explained to us. "The Aboriginal perspective is that there is creative ability in every human being in some form or another. That is one of the outcomes of living in an egalitarian society. These societies tend to teach and learn through demonstration and observation. A chief, for example, may model desired behaviors and lead with kind of a moral authority, but he or she doesn't have any right to order people around. In these kinds of societies, it's a given that everyone has something to contribute. Whether it is a child or someone who doesn't have high social standing, it doesn't matter, they all have something significant to contribute to the community."

Dr. Brokenleg also emphasizes that living in a diverse society helps each person form and experience his or her own sense of uniqueness. "Power lies in that uniqueness. Out of that is going to be a different perspective, and therein lies creativity. It's the benefit of being with people who are different from oneself."

So what does this mean for education and classroom learning? Because we all are uniquely different in our abilities, interests, passions, and the ways in which we come to understand the world around us, our school systems have to become more skillful, much more nimble and flexible, and knowledgeable about how to identify the way in which individual students learn. We can then use that in an informed way to personalize the learning.

HOW TO MOVE BEYOND DIVERSITY TO INCLUSIVITY

So how do we embrace diversity and embed it into our school districts and organizations so that we can all benefit from the creativity it fosters? I believe we need to move beyond diversity to a concept of inclusivity.

First, encouraging underrepresented groups to reach the top ranks is well-intentioned and has many valuable benefits beyond fostering a condition for creativity. This needs to continue. We also need to reexamine how people are expected to make that climb to the top, to ensure there is not a one-ladder-fits-all pathway.

This brings me to the most critical point of all: When it comes to creativity, executive teams don't need to wait until someone is in the boardroom to benefit from their ideas. We need to realize that leadership and innovation exist at all levels in a corporation, in all individuals, and not just at the top. If conditions are embedded to bring each individual's own brilliance to light, then the organization will vastly increase its knowledge, skills, and innovative and productive capacities. This same concept applies to a classroom.

In other words, we need to build on our efforts to increase and value diversity by evolving to a philosophy of *inclusivity*. As the word implies, inclusivity values and includes every individual.

Whereas Nellie's example outlines a business scenario, I believe similar goals are held within our school systems. In our quest to increase outcomes and productivity, societies have come to believe that a top-down system, although not perfect, is at least effective and efficient. But to get creativity and innovation from all your employees, teachers, and students, it's well worth the effort to move to inclusivity. Moreover, this creates a sense of belonging, another critical condition for supporting creativity.

SO HOW CAN YOU ENCOURAGE THE KIND OF INCLUSIVITY THAT DRIVES REAL INNOVATIVE CHANGE IN AN ORGANIZATION?

Celebrate the Unique Capacities of Every Individual

A leadership philosophy that celebrates the unique capacities of *every* individual is a powerful way to embrace diversity, strengthen a community, and increase morale. A group that can draw from different skill sets, backgrounds, and life experiences can provide a broader range of ideas and contributions than a more homogenous group. At the same time, morale goes up when teachers, students, and the community feel they are all in a safe, welcoming environment. A culture of inclusivity naturally seeks out the potential that lies in all. This includes the concept that abilities, knowledge, and skills change over the course of a lifetime, and this provides more diversity, leadership, and creativity, not less.

We talked to Anna-Karina Tabunar, the creator of *Talent Untapped*, a documentary that tells the story of people who have struggled mightily with a range of disabilities and how they surmounted those challenges by honing their unique talents.

Anna-Karina was at the top of her career, the spokesperson for Canada's aviation security agency, and a mom with three busy kids. Then one morning she woke up with a bad headache. Within a few days, more disturbing symptoms appeared, with swollen fingers and feet and strange patches of numbness in her limbs and face.

"I realized something was wrong when I looked down and I couldn't see the ground," says Anna-Karina. "I went to the doctor, and she wrote on the prescription pad the word 'neurological.' I couldn't believe it. I was healthy, I was doing yoga, but there was something wrong with my brain and nervous system."

So started a journey through the medical system of tests, MRIs, and CT scans, while Anna-Karina's symptoms worsened. "My legs were heavy, I had to literally lift my legs with my hands to get up the stairs. I had no sensation in my face, and my hands had this tingling and numbing."

Finally, the diagnosis came in as a rare variant of Guillain-Barré syndrome, which triggers the immune system to attack the peripheral nervous system. In Anna-Karina's case, it also included her optic nerves. "I couldn't see the details of faces. I couldn't read. My vision was terribly distorted. I appeared normal, but I could no longer do what I had been doing for a living. I was considered disabled."

Anna-Karina decided to turn her hand to volunteer work, but it wasn't easy. A seven-minute walk took her more than an hour, and reading was extremely difficult. But as she began to recover and gained confidence, she noticed she was surrounded by people who were blind, had low vision, or had other disabilities.

"I realized there is a whole community out there, other people who are so educated, so tech savvy, who are getting along and who were teaching me how to use voice-to-text and all these accessible features on my iPhone and iPad. They were my teachers, but they were unemployed. It opened my eyes to this demographic that is highly underutilized."

Anna-Karina felt a calling to tell their story through a documentary film. Her disability did not hold her back. "I thought to myself, it will take me a bit longer, but I need to get it out there."

The public agreed. A request for crowdfunding snowballed to the point the project attracted funding from private citizens, nonprofit organizations, and corporations around the world. Anna-Karina was determined to reveal the leadership brilliance of this often-overlooked sector of society. "In my mind, it had to be done. I was going to see it through."

Today, as Anna-Karina continues her recovery, she leads an organization that tours the country to help organizations and businesses understand the value to their companies of hiring people with disabilities. This is why her film *Talent Untapped* not only follows her journey to find answers for more inclusivity in the workplace but also serves as a tool that workplaces can use to become more inclusive. It establishes a business case about how adding people with disabilities to an organization creates a better workforce. It also shares a number of success stories of how people with disabilities found meaningful work and the beneficial impact this had on their organizations.

There are critical lessons here to be considered from the perspective of our schools and classrooms. It is so easy when dealing with youngsters with disabilities to allow that to become the point of focus. Some years ago, during a presentation, I mistakenly introduced a high school teacher as a teacher for autistic children. She was offended but interrupted me in the nicest of ways to explain to the assembled audience that this was a common error. She corrected me and informed me she was a teacher of children with autism. The shift in emphasis is profound. I had identified them first by their disability. I was mortified and have been careful never to make the mistake again.

RECOGNIZE THAT LEADERSHIP COMES FROM ALL LEVELS

Increasing diversity and inclusivity in leadership is an area that could profoundly benefit from taking a strength-based approach. Current efforts to foster diversity instead approach the issue as a problem and then attempt to solve the problem: We don't have enough X, Y, and Z in upper management—we need to get more.

The problem with this deficit-based approach is that, in its linear fashion, it doesn't go nearly far enough. As Nellie discovered, it attempts to embrace change by taking today's culture and processes—that is, the concept that an organization's decisions are made and ideas formed by MBA executives sitting around a boardroom table on the top floor—and catapults it into the future, by putting *different* MBA executives around a boardroom table on the top floor. Whereas some diversity and new ideas might be achieved through this approach, which is a good start, it won't be enough to build the foundation of a truly creative and inclusive organization.

CELEBRATE THE FIRST AGE THAT IS TRULY INCLUSIVE OF EVERYBODY

Past ages tended to favor some groups of workers, and students, over others. In the late 1990s, for example, many employers actively sought to recruit and promote younger employees with the idea that these "digital natives" were more technologically savvy. This worked to disengage, devalue, and demotivate older employees, who usually form the majority of a company's workforce.

Refreshingly, the age of creativity is inclusive of everyone, because every person has creative ideas and leadership capabilities to offer. Taking a strength-based approach with inclusivity recognizes that every person, at every level of an organization, possesses informal leadership abilities, creative capacities, individual talents, unique knowledge, and innovative thinking.

FLATTEN YOUR HIERARCHIES: EXPAND LEADERSHIP HORIZONTALLY AND VERTICALLY

At the school board where I worked, we took this different approach. We viewed the organization like a living organism, made up of an intricate and interdependent balance of subsystems. If we allowed even one part to languish, then all the subsystems would be diminished—including the formal leadership. It would be like thinking the brain and the rest of the body will be fine even if the heart is malfunctioning.

To expand our culture of leadership and optimize the creative learning environments throughout our school district, we knew we had to take a holistic view and pay attention to all the different elements and all the people who held a stake in what we accomplished.

This included expanding leadership not only vertically to every staff member and student in our district but also horizontally, into the broader community. We knew that students and teachers have a better chance of thriving if parents, partners, businesses, organizations, and the greater community are thriving as well. I will say it again—in this age of complexity, education is far too complicated to lay on the shoulders of a single teacher in the classroom.

Moreover, thanks to communications technology and an increasingly interconnected global marketplace, we knew our school board could have a positive influence not only beyond its walls but even beyond borders. As part of a "web of subsystems" connected to businesses, governments, social agencies, nonprofits, and other educational systems, the OCDSB could bring people together and facilitate community engagement, personal development, and broader social change.

One of our OCDSB school principals, Shannon Smith, found that building connections with the community can increase school morale even during challenging times. When her elementary school transitioned to seventh and eighth grades only, three-quarters of the students arriving on the first day of school were new—as well as many of the teachers.

"They say it takes a village to raise a child, and I wanted to hold an open house to show these new families that we're all about community involvement,"

Shannon says. "I reached out to about 30 community partners, such as our ski program, a local fitness club, our tennis club, the public health nurse, our social worker, and local businesses so we could have display booths and tons of hands-on activities."

Shannon was overwhelmed by the positive response. "More than 250 people came, and we only have about 190 students. Everyone wanted to see what this whole community school thing was all about. We began building a culture that night and it gave everyone a sense of belonging."

Today, the school holds "Meet the Community" events at the beginning of each year, expanding the traditional "meet the staff" to include the broader community.

"Our staff and students benefit from the involvement of individuals and organizations that otherwise might not be part of the school, such as two retired engineers who come three times per week to run our extracurricular robotics, 3D printing, and computer coding clubs," says Shannon. "These volunteers had no connection to the school other than living nearby and a desire to foster these skills in youngsters. They work with staff to find connections between what the students are learning in science, math, and art in order to expand on those concepts in the clubs. Had it not been for that initial open house, we may never have connected with them."

Another teacher, Andrea Jensen, found that fostering these connections also energized people in the community. "It makes people feel good to know others are interested in their work and they can contribute to students' learning," she says. "We have a local potter who is like a resident artist for our school. She is also part of the panel judging the students' portfolios."

Andrea also describes the educational and inspirational value of taking students out into the community. "We take an annual field trip to the potter's farm to learn the art of Raku firing. This trip is so popular that parents and previous students come back a second and even a third time. At the farm, the young artists watch as their work is fired in an outdoor kiln. They watch as chaos and science form into organic waves and turn their work into masterpieces. That's when they're hooked: on art, on science, and on the artists that make up their community. It's like there are no more walls; it's a semipermeable membrane the school has."

EXPAND YOUR EXPECTATIONS
WITH A GROWTH MIND-SET

I was recently making polite small talk regarding a lovely couple, who happen to be residents of a retirement home.

"They don't like to throw anything away," their son said to me. "That's because they were brought up during the Great Depression."

From the greatest generation to baby boomers to millennials, it's a common notion that each generation is shaped by the experiences of its youth. But when having this conversation, it suddenly struck me as an odd way of thinking. This couple had lived through some seven decades since the Depression—were all their habits and character traits really so thoroughly and permanently formed and entrenched by the experiences of their first decade? Didn't the following seven decades have any impact on their wisdom and beliefs?

Another colleague told me a story about a whitepaper draft he'd been asked to critique. In it, a survey had asked a range of customers how often they performed online transactions such as paying bills, paying mortgages, getting loans, automated paycheck deposits, paying into retirement savings plans, and the like. The results revealed that younger patrons, on average, made about three times more online transactions a month than older patrons.

"Aha!" the whitepaper crowed. "We can conclude that older generations are less likely to use online transactions, due to their 'fear' of technology, and we should focus services on a younger audience."

My friend explains, "They were so eager to draw this commonly held myth, that older people fear technology, that they overlooked the fact that the entire sample surveyed was made up from a list of people who *all* used online transactions in the first place. And the reason the older generation had less online transactions per month wasn't because they were afraid to use the technology but because they no longer had a need for the services in the survey—they had finished paying their mortgage, they no longer worked or paid into RSPs, and weren't in need of loans."

In fact, some of the elder population actually appreciated using online banking due to mobility and driving issues, making them a prime market for more online services. But this potential market was overlooked due to the eagerness to label and categorize people by age.

Too often, we have preconceived notions of what people are like or what they think and feel—based on anything from the generation in which they were born to where they grew up. Not only do we risk misconceptions with these stereotypes, but we also overlook the fact that people continue to grow well beyond their early years. Learning is, after all, a lifelong process!

ENGAGE YOUR TEACHERS AND STUDENTS IN BROADER, EXCITING COMMUNITIES

Connecting with the broader community can also provide real-world experiences for students while allowing teachers to interact with peers, making their day more stimulating as well.

In teacher Kent Van Dyk's culinary arts class, for example, chefs are brought into the classroom from up to 250 miles away. "The students will work with the chef to create a dish, which is then served at one of our Gala Evenings, attended by some 120 members of the community," says Van Dyk. The galas and other catering events generate income for the program, as well as for one local and one international charity each year. Van Dyk is also making plans to tap into the knowledge of local cheese makers, bakeries, restaurant owners, and senior citizens in the area.

Schools can build positive energy both horizontally across the community and vertically into the future. Our interactions with our students, employees, and community connections hold tremendous power. The positive things we give them to take forward can lay the foundation for an entire community's engagement, morale, and success.

BRING PEOPLE FROM ALL LEVELS INTO YOUR BOARDROOM AND LEADERSHIP CONFERENCES

There is no need to have people climb the corporate ladder before you invite them into your boardroom to share their ideas and knowledge or invite them to participate or present at your leadership conferences. Remember that a successful leader is not someone who simply provides direction. The new leader, whether formal or informal, is one who facilitates the success of others, by mentoring, motivating, and inspiring them to their highest potential.

In our Lead the Way campaign, one of our goals was to promote our understanding that every student, employee, parent, volunteer, and community member connected to our organization is a leader. This aligned nicely with what we were doing in our classrooms—helping our students to become leaders in their learning. Lead the Way became an important mechanism to bring people from all employee groups together to learn and celebrate the contributions they are making, directly or indirectly, to teaching and learning in our school district.

EMBRACE NEW FORMS OF LEADERSHIP

Similarly, leadership and ideas must be encouraged from all levels of an organization, as well as from outside of it as districts collaborate and form partnerships with the broader community.

At the OCDSB, custodian Stan Baines, who copresented with me and another school superintendent at an Australian conference on leadership, says, "A school is a much better place for all, especially the students, when staff are considered peers and equals."

In one of the schools at which Stan worked, custodians are actively involved in school life, doing video yearbooks, making morning announcements, and organizing student events and sports.

"From library techs to administrators, people are breaking out of their defined labels and into more integrated roles," says Stan. "This is invigorating, giving people the chance to try new things and develop their interests and knowledge."

Stan adds that the more involved the auxiliary staff is, the more aware the students are of their importance to the school. "It gives the school a more comfortable atmosphere because nobody is a stranger. The whole school is a classroom, and everyone there plays a role in a child's education. People are more than just a job title; they are role models."

LEARN MORE ABOUT THE INDIVIDUALS IN YOUR ORGANIZATION—AND DON'T BE AFRAID TO ASK THE TOUGH QUESTIONS

How do your students feel about bullying, sexual orientation, or their families? Do they feel a sense of belonging in their school? Do they feel welcomed, valued, and respected? How does your staff feel about leadership and developmental opportunities? How many people in your organization speak a second language?

Taking surveys to understand the demographic and sociographic context of your student and staff population helps to shine light on perspectives, issues, and opportunities. This information can also lead to amazing ideas for events that bring the community together in the fullness of its diversity and inclusivity.

One Lead the Way event, led by Jacqueline Lawrence, coordinator of diversity and inclusion at the OCDSB, was called A Date with Diversity and invited some 300 staff members, parents, and community partners from a wide variety of backgrounds to share their stories and experiences. "It helped us foster a sense of belonging," Lawrence says. "Schools are on the front lines of social change, so we have a lot to teach about diversity."

CELEBRATE INCLUSIVITY BOLDLY AND VISIBLY

Fostering inclusive leadership must be celebrated, boldly and visibly. Lead the Way events provided engaging opportunities for these celebrations and became microcosms of inclusivity in themselves. They were attended not just by school employees but also by students, parents, and partners such as businesses, government agencies, universities and colleges, nonprofits, hospitals, police services, arts and science organizations, the trades, and many others. Lead the Way events were also designed to give voices from all walks of life in the community a chance to speak, including students as young as age six.

PROVIDE REASSURANCE AND ENCOURAGE COLLABORATION

The idea of flattened hierarchies can be frightening to some. I have two tips to help secure buy-in. First, involve as many people as possible, both inside and outside the district. People are less likely to fear something they've collaborated on. At the same time, the more individuals and groups involved, the greater the momentum to push forward.

Second, engage experts. For the OCDSB, the benefit of consulting with a variety of experts was twofold: It allowed us to cost-effectively access a wealth of resources and techniques to catalyze cultural shifts, and the professional presenters helped build momentum, understanding, credibility, and above all, fun and enthusiasm.

As we've said before, education is too complex to rest solely in the hands of a teacher in a classroom. The more successfully we can harness the unique and diverse capacities within our students, employee groups, parents, volunteers, and community partners, both local and global, the more opportunity we will have to bring out the brilliance of every child in our care. The goal is to continue to collaborate and share our findings, and everyone is invited to join in.

Once you recognize that creative capacity and leadership abilities exist in every person, regardless of rank or background, you have a better understanding of the power of not just diversity but inclusivity and how to foster an environment that supports a culture of engagement and belonging. You will need to boldly break down walls and form partnerships outside of the organization, letting the outside world in and going out into the community to tap into new resources.

Stories From the Field

Teaching Teachers to Foster Sustainable Communities

If we're going to move toward inclusivity, which ultimately supports the imperatives for establishing cultures of belonging and recognizing that seed of brilliance in everyone, then a great place to start is in the classrooms—the classrooms where we teach teachers.

Michael Wilson, a retired arts education professor at the University of Ottawa in Ottawa, Canada, was able to witness the value of this firsthand. "Due to a new mandate from the provincial ministry of education, we needed to place each of the incoming candidates for our Bachelor of Education program in a cohort, or specialized area of study," he says. "We came up with the cohorts of comprehensive school health, developing global perspectives, French as a second language, and urban education. I then suggested a cohort for imagination, creativity, and innovation and was surprised when it was accepted."

One of the benefits of the cohorts, according to Wilson, was to provide applicants with "a unique opportunity to work with a team of education leaders who have strong research relationships and professional partnerships with different local, national, and international communities," with a mission to "prepare teachers to educate students . . . for the ethical, societal, and technological demands necessary toward fostering sustainable 21st-century communities."

Michael planned to model the new community-building imagination, creativity, and innovation cohort after the work he'd seen Peter Gamwell lead at the Ottawa-Carleton District School Board. The name was chosen to highlight the process from imagination to creativity to innovation, but the acronym ICI is also French for the word *here* and is also used as a short form for "come here." The acronym thus captured not only the bilingual nature of the university but also created an inviting reference to inclusivity.

Although the name was delightfully warm and clever, there were plenty of less pleasant surprises in store for the budding cohort program. "We loved the idea, but no one knew how we were going to realize imagination, creativity, and innovation as a blueprint for teacher education," says Michael.

But as a jazz musician, Michael felt that a certain amount of improvisation would be normal. "By definition, spontaneous creativity means you do not know what the next moment is going to be like, and so part of the process is learning to live with that sense of uncertainty. The first surprise we had was a very pleasant one—the various cohort programs were opened to registration and the candidate response to our cohort was astounding. We were full within two weeks after the registration announcement was made, with a long waiting list."

(Continued)

(Continued)

Now it was time to actually "get with the program," which proved more difficult. "We decided to give our candidates some experiences in creativity, imagination, and innovation and from those experiences try to extrapolate those elements for their gained wisdom and knowledge. In other words, we would start with the experience and talk about it later. I had thought about the candidates working in small groups, in kind of independent field studies with schools."

Then the second, not so pleasant surprise happened. "Halfway through the course, I realized I didn't get the proper permissions to carry out such a project. So we were suddenly stuck with an entire cohort being unable to do part of their program. Under normal circumstances, I would have organized some kind of equivalent assignment. But when I told students what happened, I learned leadership does come from all levels. They suggested I let them come up with alternative assignments to meet the criteria of the course. I agreed. To my astonishment, they all came up with very different ideas. Their ideas were far more interesting and fascinating and innovative than anything I could have dreamed up."

Try This!

Fun Plus One

Help flatten your hierarchies by making your leadership events or developmental activities a "plus one." Every time your school or organization holds a leadership or professional development day, mandate as many participants as possible to bring a guest. Who they bring is their choice, but it must be someone who

a) is a student, parent, or volunteer;

b) works in a different department within the board than the person issuing the invitation;

c) is from the greater community, for example, in business, medicine, technology, or science; and

d) holds a very different viewpoint from the person issuing the invitation.

7 Condition #3: Making It Personal

"Kids have to have a direction for their talents,
otherwise they don't know what to do."

—Michael Caine (2011)

When I was at school, we had two social studies teachers. One would enter the room with binders that he had compiled, presumably during his youth at university. He read them to us. Literally. For two years. I've often thought that he must have been the only person in the world who 1) kept his binders and 2) whose binders weren't dusty.

So immersed was he in this process that it allowed us time to hone our own skills with a variety of cleverly designed paper missile launchers. We became very accurate. We had to. Because we were, as Elliot Eisner (1985) once said about all humankind, stimulus-seeking missiles. We needed novelty. And it wasn't coming from the teacher.

Our other social studies teacher was somewhat older. He would amble in, more often than not fairly disheveled, sometimes wearing what appeared to be his slippers. He would plunk himself into a seat and proceed to fascinate us with his knowledge of economics and world affairs. He used stories to illustrate the concepts. He was brilliant. He needed no notes. They were stored in his mind, along with the fluid ability to illustrate with endless anecdotes.

I've already discussed the importance of storytelling as a condition for creativity in Chapter 5. But what made this teacher a true sower of conditions of creativity is that he could personalize his stories to each and every one of us, in a way that would make sense to us.

One day, this particular teacher was conducting a lesson on diminishing marginal utility. Suddenly, he turned to me and said, "Gamwell, you appear confused."

"I am, sir."

"And what might be the source of your confusion on this occasion?"

"Diminishing marginal utility, sir."

"What is it you don't understand?"

"Diminishing marginal utility, sir."

"Do you like beans, Gamwell?"

"Like what, sir?"

"*Beans*, boy. Do you like beans? You know, those things you eat with bacon and eggs—they come out of a can—Heinz makes them!"

"Yes sir, I do."

As a teenage boy, he had hit on a topic very close to my heart. Food, and protein-rich beans especially. My interest was piqued—I was awakened— beans! Economics was now all about beans. I must, I decided, look into this as a potential career.

"Tell me, when you dig into your plate, and take that first mouthful, explain the experience."

"They're delicious, sir."

"On a scale of one to ten, how delicious?"

"Twelve, sir!"

"And then the second mouthful. How does that taste?"

"Delicious, sir."

"On a scale of one to ten. How delicious?"

"Hmm. Ten, sir."

"Is the second mouthful as delicious as the first?"

Pause.

"Probably not, sir."

"And the third mouthful?"

"Perhaps a seven, sir."

"All right then. That's diminishing marginal utility."

Had the teacher written the term *diminishing marginal utility* on the chalkboard and its definition next to it, I can assure you I wouldn't have remembered it or understood it. But the way he related it to a story about beans means I've never forgotten it—and I bet you will never forget it now either. That's the beauty of personalized learning.

IS YOUR SCHOOL OR BUSINESS
A SAUSAGE-MAKING FACTORY?

In 2014, I was presenting along with a couple of colleagues about fostering creative organizations at the International Principals' Conference in Cairns, Australia. The keynote speaker was Yong Zhao. Yong is the presidential chair and director of the Institute for Global and Online Education in the College of Education, University of Oregon, as well as a professor in the Department of Educational Measurement, Policy, and Leadership. I was captured by his very creative and succinct vision for schools, for which he had only one criteria: Get my kid out of my basement!

The problem, he claimed, is that schools are actually like sausage makers. There is lots of accountability for them to produce the best sausages they can, but they are all the same sausages. In this new complex age when creativity is so crucial, and where diversity is imperative, we need new ways to allow students' unique capacities to flourish.

So What Ought to Be Our Priorities?

Don't just personalize it—make it personal. There has been a lot of great discussion about personalized learning, but I would like to take it one step further and say I believe we also need to make it personal. We have to actually make it matter to the student. I'll describe how with a few examples shortly.

LOOK AT THE POWER OF THE APOSTROPHE TO CHANGE THE WORLD

For a host of reasons, education systems developed to prioritize certain aspects of human intelligence. Language, reading, writing, and mathematics are critical skills. I kept a pretty close eye on my own children's performance in these areas! But equally important is the priority to find the unique talents of our students and ways to spark their interests and passions.

One of the things we need to balance is the tendency to focus our attention on the performance of the collective, meaning students' achievement, as opposed to moving the apostrophe one space to the left to focus on an individual student's achievement. For me, this is a crucial distinction.

Throughout my career, I've witnessed how the real magic occurs when we recognize that within every child lies the seeds of potential, of possibility, of brilliance. This sets in place the processes and pathways—and the conditions— to reveal the uniqueness within each of them. The imperative is to create the conditions under which the abilities and interests of individual students emerge naturally in a supportive, nonjudgmental learning environment. We need to figure out what they are good at, including those abilities that lie beyond the core basics, and grow them from there. It's called personalization.

TAKE MORE TIME

And I think we need to slow down a little bit. At the beginning of this book, we talked at length about the frantic, complex, swirling pace of our society. We need to take care that we don't get overwhelmed by this and to take our time with our students' learning in our classrooms. Difficult as it may be, we can strive to be more mindful and to infuse our learning environments with calm. Our children need that. It is a crazy world sometimes. We need to find the balance between fostering resiliency and protecting the vulnerability of young minds.

THE ANCIENT WISDOM OF THE CHINESE BAMBOO TREE

MY STORY, OUR STORY

By Jacqueline Lawrence

A circle expands to welcome, to honour,
To connect me to the genius within.
In my mind, in my heart, in my dreams,
I carry seeds of greatness.
They wait for you.
Every word you speak waters them
Every thought you hold nurtures them
Every silent hush whispers them to me
In the darkness when I do not believe
They still live inside me.
In five years
We will know
How tall we grow
You are my present
I am your future
In five years
We will know
We will know
How tall we grow.

The ancient story of how bamboo grows provides insight into our students' seeds of brilliance and how we must be patient. As the story goes, for the first year after the bamboo seed is planted, nothing grows above the ground. Nothing grows the second year either. Or the third. Or the fourth. Now if you were a bamboo farmer, you might be tempted to dig that seed up out of the ground and see what the heck is wrong with it. But then you would fail to see the miracle that bursts forth in the fifth year, when the bamboo plant grows 80 feet in a single season.

It's a wonderful reminder that if we set the right conditions, then cultivate carefully, learning and growth will flourish.

SEE LEARNING AS "DIFFERENCE THAT MAKES A DIFFERENCE"

For many years I have been fascinated by the thinking and work of Gregory Bateson. I've been reading one of his books, *Steps to an Ecology of Mind*, since 1985. It's pretty intense stuff, which is why it's taken me so long.

Bateson (1972) was one of the first people to bring cybernetic thinking to the social sciences, and he is often cited as having defined information as "difference that makes a difference." It struck me one day that the definition is equally valid for learning. Learning is difference that makes a difference.

The best way I know to make learning make a difference to students is to ensure it is personalized. That the "stuff" of learning connects to the learner. This goes beyond just personalization, to making things personal. The learning must *matter* to them. If it does not matter, then it's unlikely to make a difference to them, and learning is equally unlikely to occur.

The very best teachers and leaders, be it in a family, a classroom, an electrical company, a hospital—wherever—accomplish this with fluidity. They manage to organize the tasks and set in place the cultural conditions that have to be accomplished in a way that everyone's abilities and interests are sparked.

Interestingly, this works on an individual, group, organizational, and, I believe, societal level. The goal is optimal learning. Or as the famous psychologist Mihály Csíkszentmihályi calls it, flow—that amazing experience when you become so immersed in what you are doing that you feel a buzz in your mind and lose total track of time.

Csíkszentmihályi identifies a number of elements involved in achieving flow:

- Clear goals are set throughout
- Immediate feedback is available
- Challenges and skills are evenly balanced
- Action and awareness are merged
- No distractions
- No worry of failure
- No self-consciousness

- Sense of time becomes distorted
- The activity becomes an end in itself

The first time I heard of Csíkszentmihályi, I was perusing a local bookstore and came across *Finding Flow*. At first, I was delighted to have found what I thought was the female equivalent of *Where's Waldo*. But my disappointment in my mistake was short-lived once I was introduced to his work. Csíkszentmihályi used a now quite famous study called the Beeper Test, or the Experience Sampling Study. He attached beepers to people from a wide array of working environments and beeped them throughout the day. I'd have loved the chance to do that to some of my coworkers! Anyway, each time he beeped them, he asked them to respond to a series of questions, some as simple as how are you feeling, and what are you doing?

Csíkszentmihályi found when people were engaged in activities that were very challenging, but their ability to accomplish the task matched the level of the challenge, they reported feeling engaged and content. This experience he labeled flow.

The interesting thing about flow, which some people call buzz and what I refer to as optimal learning, is that people experiencing it report feelings of well-being and happiness. Learning and work become an enjoyable experience, and indeed time flies. This experience, I believe, is the holy grail of learning.

Whereas we have all experienced optimal learning, we do so in different ways and through different activities. This is because we are all so unique, with particular interests, abilities, and creative capacities. Some experience flow playing sports or music, but it can occur in all realms of life. Plumbing, gardening, building, brainstorming, accounting, organizing closets; it depends on our interests and passions.

Another curious thing about flow is that, like our interests, it is likely to shift and change throughout our lives. For example, say you were to go back and ask my teachers about my areas of interest. (For many reasons I would ask you not to do that. Many of my teachers have passed on, and those still with us might join them at the mention of my name.) They might have thought of music and drama as two of my special interests, but I can assure you none of them would have envisioned my passion for research and thinking. So we have to be careful not to jump to conclusions about labeling our youngsters.

As we come to a deeper understanding about the conditions under which learning and creativity flourish, I believe the implications of flow are significant not only for individual learning but also for group learning and organizational and societal learning. For me, it provides a unique lens through which to assess learning environments.

Stories From the Field

Helping Reluctant Readers Start a New Chapter

An important thing to understand about personalized learning is it's not just about letting a student choose his or her own topic for a project. It's about taking the time to get to know what is deeply meaningful to the student—and allowing that student to learn in a meaningful way that makes sense to him or her.

And that isn't always going to be pretty.

Teacher and author Allison van Diepen has a keen understanding of this aspect of personalized learning. She's written several teenage novels described in reviews as "one hell of a page-turner" and "A . . . gritty tale of the streets with genuine heart." Her action-packed thrillers have been lauded by ALA Quick Picks for Reluctant Readers and New York City Public Library Books for the Teen Age. (She also includes comprehensive study guides for teachers on her website, which you'll want to check out if you choose to study one of her novels in your class.)

But whereas Allison loves reading and writing today, it wasn't always that way. I asked her to tell me her story and how she had found her passion—and it was not a linear path.

"Growing up, I didn't think books were fun," Allison says. "I was a reluctant reader, more interested in watching movies and TV."

Then, when she was about 12, Allison's sister introduced her to Goosebumps books and other teen thrillers. She went from being a nonreader to an avid one and soon began developing her own story ideas.

She was encouraged by a teacher.

Allison explains, "For an assignment, I wrote a story called *The Obsession*, about a teenage girl who was being stalked by a psychotic killer. The teacher wrote, 'I expect you'll see your name on the cover of a book one day.' That comment was life changing. It's the only written comment that I ever remembered from a teacher."

Over the next few years, Allison wrote several other manuscripts. Her goal was to become a published author, and she stayed up late on weekends to write. Her mother became her sounding board.

"My mom let me read stories to her and I would see her reactions. She would laugh or cry or be horrified, and that bolstered my

(Continued)

(Continued)

confidence. She had such faith in me. She still does. She's still my first editor."

Allison naturally chose to study English at university but was disappointed. "They treated the arts like sciences," she says. "They took the fun away, the magic out. It was boring. I got my first C."

Fortunately, Allison found the drama she was looking for by picking up history. "It was fascinating to learn how people lived and what they went through hundreds of years ago. That inspired me. I thought I'd write historical fiction."

After graduating, Allison went to teachers' college. She landed a teaching job in Brooklyn, New York, at a school that stretched an entire city block with 4,000 students. It was a school with metal detectors on the doors and many students who were gang members.

"In the classroom, I noticed these students weren't reading what they were supposed to be reading," says Allison. "They were street books, urban fiction, or 'hood lit.' They depicted urban life in gritty, explicit ways, with lots of violence and sex. But the students enjoyed them. And I could see why. The realities of Brooklyn life—their lives—were reflected in those books. That's why they chose them."

These weren't the type of books you wanted a young teen reading. However, rather than try to force the students to read more traditional works, Allison decided to do what she could to make available reading materials more personal and meaningful for these students. "I decided to write a book for my students that would capture their realities in a story they could relate to but would be more appropriate for a teenage audience."

That book was *Street Pharm*, about a teenage drug dealer named Ty Johnson whose father, a drug kingpin, is in prison.

Says Allison, "Many of the students were real smart, charismatic kids, with tons of potential. With Ty, I was trying to get into their heads. My main goal was to entertain teens and to make them love reading, as well as get them thinking about the issues."

Allison has written almost a dozen books now, and the feedback from her readers shows how personalization can transform a student's engagement for a subject matter. "The feedback I often hear is, 'I thought I hated reading, but then I read your books.' We all have different gifts. Some of those are shown in the classroom and some are not, but discovering those gifts is critical to a student's future and their happiness."

PERSONALIZED LEARNING THROUGH ROCK OPERAS

As I mentioned earlier, when I taught in Newfoundland and Labrador, I used to put on rock operas. Not by myself, of course. There were a lot of us. But I did most of the music and a lot of the directing, and a host of others became involved in a range of other tasks crucial to the growing of a production.

Artists created banners, carpenters and designers worked on sets, costume makers worked their magic, and the science-oriented people made weird and wonderful stuff happen. For one of the rock operas we put on, written by me and a friend, the second act took place in a space observatory that slowly descended from the heavens. A group of 10 staff members and some students got together on a weekend, borrowed some framing metal beams from a local garden center, and created a massive space dome.

But now we had a problem. I asked, "How the hell are we going to get that up into the rafters of the auditorium? If it falls down, we'll kill someone!"

"Gamwell, do we interfere with your stuff? Do we interrupt your music and acting? No. So go home and leave us alone!"

Sure enough, at the appointed hour, the magnificent dome descended, turning gracefully as it did so, eventually coming to rest on the stage as the final notes of the scene's music drifted away. It was a memorable scene—and no injuries.

So what did I learn? First, people are at their best when they are working from an area of strength. The reason our productions were so good was people involved themselves in things that were personally interesting to them and that mattered to them personally. The scenery was incredible, because the people building it were passionate about what they did. They became obsessed with ensuring perfection, not only in the building but in rehearsing the set changes. Everything was timed perfectly.

I also learned that once you've figured out the broad strokes of what you want to achieve, allow people to make sense of it themselves. With the rock operas, once we'd mapped out the overall scope of the scenes and the ideas behind the vision, then it was best to get out of people's way and let them figure out how they would achieve it. Don't disappear—stay around and offer your insight when asked, but don't micromanage. This allows each individual to contribute his or her own ideas and capabilities to the result, and trust me, you will be surprised by the magic.

The rock operas were my first experience of leading learning experiences that exhibited the key features of flow, or optimized learning. In the first production we created, *Jesus Christ Superstar*, optimized learning occurred in many ways and had impacts on the individual, group, and organizational levels, as well as on the greater community.

Because the participants were engaged in personalized areas of passion, interest, and ability, they found their own flow. They didn't want to leave school at the end of the day. And oftentimes, no one had known beforehand these students had these abilities. In one production, a student playing a lead role had spent much of his school life in special education classes. His participation in the opera transformed the way he saw himself and how others saw him. It was powerful and moving to behold.

FROM ROCK OPERAS TO THE CLASSROOM

The experience of producing these rock operas fermented in my mind for a long time. They so resonated with the people involved. Students who might otherwise be first to leave school each day willingly stayed behind long after everyone had left. To sing, to dance, to build, to plan, to paint.

They broke down the barriers of conventional relationships. Cliques all but disappeared. We had students from very different socioeconomic, social, and academic backgrounds connecting in some very profound ways.

Many answers came to my mind about why these rock operas had such a profound effect, but each answer came with more questions. So I started to use some of the same approaches that characterized the productions in my teaching practice. No matter what the topic, I tried to figure out the interests and abilities of the students and create novel, surprising ways for them to engage with the learning experiences through their own particular abilities.

If kids became so passionately interested in such things that they didn't want to leave school, how could I bring this magic to the classroom? So was born the idea for a study. I was already using many of the ideas; I just wanted to formalize it. I applied to the University of Ottawa to start a PhD program. A key element of this involved an action research study that examined the experiences of intermediate students as I taught them their language and literature curriculum using the arts as a catalyst for learning.

THE MUSICAL SOUNDTRACK STORIES PROJECT

One project in which I engaged the students was called musical soundtrack stories. I asked each student to choose a piece of classical music about three minutes long. For the first week, I asked them to listen to the music over and over, so they came to know it by heart—the form, the shape, the dynamics, everything about it. Then I asked them to interpret that music in a way that made sense to and mattered to them.

Of course, initially my exciting project was met with a chorus of boos, and questions like, "What do you mean, sir? I have no idea what you're talking about."

Try this, I told them. "Close your eyes and listen to your piece of music again. This time, allow your mind to wander, to create images of what the music represents to you. What does it make you think of? How does it make you feel? Then think of how you could represent those ideas. Perhaps it's a story, a piece of art, a dance, a sculpture, or a video. Whatever. Then spend two weeks creating that representation."

I set a series of dates when the kids would bring in the artifacts of their learning and then moved aside and let them go at it. I put on a confident and encouraging smile, although deep down I wasn't sure how the project was going to turn out.

I needn't have worried. What occurred was a blossoming of creative ideas in all shapes and sizes. A couple of kids were skateboarders and produced a music video of their skateboarding performances. A few girls, one with a younger sister who was targeted for bullying, designed and presented a puppet show to help younger children understand the issues in an age-appropriate way. One boy created a video montage to the music of *Fanfare for the Common Man*, a series of taped television segments that, in his words, showed the contrasting passions and failures of humanity.

And then there was Ross. Early in the process, Ross had approached me privately and asked for permission to be excused from telling me the nature of his project beforehand. It was apparently based on a very private and sensitive issue for him. Well, what is the purpose of personalized learning if you can't tailor the process to the student's needs? I agreed, as long as he promised to keep a journal of his progress.

On the day appointed for the presentations of the students' work, Ross brought in a video. Without saying a word, he simply pressed play.

The music started, *Canon in D*, by Pachelbel. A beautiful, poignant version. On the screen appeared Ross, formally dressed in a starched white shirt and tie, and his face more starched and serious still. He was standing in the middle of a field, holding a bouquet of flowers. He turned, and the camera (filmed by his project partner) followed him as he walked slowly through a gate, the music playing in the background. He closed the gate, then continued his somber journey. A few moments later, it became clear he was in a cemetery. He walked slowly up and down the rows of graves and eventually came to a halt in front of one of the tombstones. He knelt down, stayed still a moment, then presented the flowers and placed them on the grave. The camera zoomed in so that all could read the name on the grave marker. Then Ross stood up and retraced his steps, walking somberly through the gate, turning and closing it with finality, and then walking off into the distance. "A Tribute to My Grandfather" appeared on the screen. The music slowly faded. There was silence in the classroom. Not a sound.

Ross's grandfather had passed away the week I had assigned the project. This was how he made sense of the music and the assignment; this mattered deeply to him.

I learned many things during the course of my study, but four key findings emerged for me.

1. *Activity*. The critical importance of engaging students physically and actively in their own learning.

2. *Emotional engagement*. Learning occurs best when we understand the connection between emotional and cognitive aspects of learning. If you have an emotional connection, it will matter to you.

3. *Social construction of meaning*. The importance of sharing your ideas and listening carefully to the ideas of others in the construction of your understanding.

4. *Choice and control*. If the learning is going to matter, then wherever possible, allow students to have significant say in what they are learning about.

If you want to bring out the best in people, set the task, preferably in a collaborative manner, put in place reasonable accountability processes, and then stand off to the side and let them make sense of the world in a way that the world makes sense to them. If you give up some control, you'll find people are incredibly creative.

Which is not to say this is easy to do. So many of our structures, processes, standards, and organizations are set up to keep people confined, to measure success within narrow parameters, and—let's face it—to make our jobs predictable and therefore supposedly easier. The problem is that life's too complex for that approach today. Current realities require every ounce of creative juice to help us forge positive pathways for both our individual and collective futures. Yes, it takes a bit more effort initially, but the end results are so much richer when we take the time to awaken possibilities, to fire enthusiasm, and to encourage people to show us their magic.

We need more Wonder Walls.

Watching Ross that day, I realized if you want real learning to take place, you must make the learning experience personally meaningful.

Learning takes place in the corporate world as well, and the best thing we can do as managers is not to manage people and projects but to lead wisely, almost from the background or offstage. Set some direction, have reasonable parameters and sensible accountability, spark people's curiosity, and then give them some autonomy to do the work their way. Clearly you need to check in every now and again to make sure things are on course, and let people know you are fascinated with the process they are going through, but leave them alone to make sense of the task in a way that the task makes sense to them.

PERSONALIZATION ACROSS THE SCHOOL DISTRICT

As described previously, one of the key elements of our Lead the Way series was to model creativity through all our events—to profile creative learning in as many ways as we possibly could. The more we could profile creativity alive and well in the real world, the more likely we would be able to model it in our learning environments across the school district.

One of the most critical things to keep in mind is that all of us have different interests, different things that appeal to us, and different ways of making sense of the world. So if we want to engage all our learners, diversity and inclusivity need to be front and center. We wanted to represent diversity of interests in our events. As people walked into the conference room, their senses were awakened with the sights and sounds of diverse projects emerging from the minds of our staff, students, and community.

GENIUS HOUR: A SMART WAY TO FOSTER CREATIVITY

One project gaining enormous momentum in schools and organizations is Genius Hour. The concept, practiced by many creative organizations, is simple. Time is put aside specifically for working on a project that sparks one's interests.

One of our teachers, Chris Hiltz, became curious about it and eventually helped foster this approach to learning within his school, across the district, and even at the provincial level. As Hiltz described it to us,

> Genius Hour really spoke to me because I don't like doing the same things every year with my students. I look to see what hooks I can find, new things I can try in my classroom incorporating interests like technology and engaging the students. Genius Hour was definitely something new. So I approached my principal with the idea, showed her a video I'd found, and said, "What do you think? Can I throw the idea out to the rest of the staff and see if anyone else would be interested?" She was so enthusiastic. No hesitation whatsoever. So I put out an e-mail to everyone in the school.

Within short order, three teachers expressed an interest to Chris, and after a couple of exploratory meetings they decided to give Genius Hour a go. After the first run-through they were hooked: "Having never done anything like this before, we just wanted to see what we could do. We were all blown away by what the students did with it. It quickly became apparent what a special idea this was."

The teachers said the approach was successful due to three key elements.

1. First and foremost, having an almost instant engagement with the students, who appreciated the opportunity to explore something so grounded in their personal interests. This resonated with me. My mind went back to the project work I had done with my own students as part of my study and the critical importance of personal choice and control over the work being done.

2. Having an allocated time for Genius Hour. Too often, schools and businesses consider being creative as a nice to have—something to spend time on once the "real work" is done. Having an allocated time for Genius Hour not only dedicated time for the project but sent the message to both students and teachers that creativity is real work— often hard work—and was to be valued.

3. Having guidance and expertise from people who could help; particularly important was validation.

As Chris says,

Providing the students with validation on what they want to learn is so important. One student was passionate about snowboarding. Normally, teachers and students might engage in conversations about mutual interests. But then the conversation reverts to history, or math, or whatever is the lesson at the moment. A boy was really keen on snowboarding and wanted to learn not only about snowboarding itself but how someone like Warren Miller can put together a snowboarding movie. And he taught himself how to do that. This is why Genius Hour is so worthwhile. It shows we want to support your learning, and this sets the project apart.

By allowing students to have choice over the specific topic under exploration, it provides a powerful tool through which teachers can launch into the curriculum in a very personal way.

Another teacher involved in Genius Hour, Tania Ovens, said some of the kids who thrived during Genius Hour were the same kids who struggled in the academic stream. "Genius Hour gave them the chance to learn about something they were interested in, and they were driven to do it. Even better, other kids would talk about their project with phrases such as 'wow, that's so cool,' giving these kids incredible peer validation. So these kids who usually struggled had an opportunity to see themselves a little bit differently and to have others see them differently."

Teacher Eleri Morgan says students were able to experience success and validation and be engaged the entire time, whereas they might not normally have had that experience. "It was so uplifting, to be able to see some of those students who can fall through the cracks just suddenly coming out to shine."

Here are just two examples of students' projects created during Genius Hour.

THE STORY OF HAYDEN AND THE RUBIK'S CUBE

Hayden had not been performing to his potential and often required redirection to stay on task. There had been several meetings with his parents, who shared the same concerns.

Then, along came Genius Hour. Hayden chose as his topic a passion very close to his heart: Rubik's Cube. It was also a topic that had sometimes created problems for him in class, for he had a tendency to focus more on his Rubik's Cube than his classwork!

Genius Hour gave him the opportunity to spend allocated time figuring out how many configurations are possible with the Cube. He also explored the following conundrum: If you were able to do one turn on the Rubik's Cube each second, how many years it would take to go through every combination of the Rubik's Cube? And he created an intriguing, memorable video that wove together mathematics and storytelling and also revealed a remarkable sense of humor.

I had the opportunity to meet Hayden with his mom and dad, Maria and Bill, and to ask their perspectives on this adventure. I asked Hayden where he had come up with the idea.

"I'd always been interested in the Rubik's Cube, but nobody seemed to really see it as a way of expressing myself. It wasn't really important to them. But this project opened up the chance for me to show this was something that was important to me and something I was passionate about.

"My video showed how long it would take you to go through every single combination on a Rubik's Cube. I had to go through the number of combinations, then work back how many seconds it would take you to go through all of them, and then see if I could put that into perspective to make it mean something."

What struck me was the incredible amount of research, across subjects, Hayden had put into his project before he could even contemplate creating the video. Take a look at Hayden's video on YouTube (enter "Hayden asks why the Rubik's Cube is so hard" in the site's search box), and I guarantee you will be amazed.

Hayden's mom, Maria, was also impressed with the mathematical understanding the project demonstrated, but that wasn't what moved her most: "I felt he was trying to tell a story. When you see the video, there is very much a creative and imaginary part to it as well as mathematical understanding. For example, he tells the part about going into space. It lent to his interest in the mathematical side, but it also brought out his storytelling skills."

The Rubik's Cube experience had a significant impact on Hayden's school experience. Teacher Eleri Morgan summed it up thus:

> He took these ideas and his research about Rubik's Cube and turned it into this fabulous stop-frame animation video that had every person who watched it on the edge of their seat. Because of this, he has completely turned around academically. He received validation from his parents, from staff, from people across the system—and all of a sudden he realized he had a lot to put out there, that he had a lot of value, and that his interests and talents have value. I think this gave him a new sense of confidence that he was able to speak up, he was able to contribute, he was able to be engaged, and he had so much opportunity.

Hayden's dad, Bill, spoke to me about the impact of this opportunity on Hayden:

> It has been one of the single most important moments in his academic career. He was kind of lost—we could see this, but it wasn't really being demonstrated anywhere.

> After he created this video, he gained a sense of pride and accomplishment. He gained a sense of position within his community. He became known as the kid who could do this. He became a lot more confident. And then he went on to do very well in the science fair and became much more engaged academically. So this had repercussions that went far, far, far beyond this project.

ALL DOLLED UP: EMERSON AND THE FASHION MANNEQUIN

When I talked to Emerson, she told me she immediately liked the Genius Hour project because "this was not like any other project where the teachers give us an outline and we have to stick to it. They basically just let us loose, to do anything we wanted. We could make something or create a product, do something about sushi if you wanted to."

As Emerson says, it was clear the freedom of choice and control over the learning was critical to her engagement from the start:

> At first, I wanted to do something about adoption because I am adopted. But then I thought, that's going to bore people. I want to grab the audience's attention! I don't want them to look away, I want their eyes focused on me when I am presenting this. And so I was thinking, OK, what can I do? Wait a second, the teacher also wanted us to educate the class through our projects. So I wanted to design an outfit. But not just any outfit. I decided to research various time periods and see what the most popular fashionable clothing was. Then I would take a piece of clothing from each time period and create one outfit.

So Emerson created her fashion mannequin, dressed in items of clothing representing each of the decades through the 20th century. She also wrote a booklet that describes the historical context for each of the items.

Emerson continued,

> I put it all together, but I was forgetting something. I needed to show the teachers I wasn't just playing dress-up with a mannequin. I needed to show I learned something throughout this process of the Genius Hour. I was thinking I am not going to do a presentation because presentations are like so blah. I mean they're fun, I like them, but I need to do something more out there. And so I made my fashion booklet.

This clearly mattered to Emerson.

Emerson's mom, Lucy, described how Emerson created the booklet:

> Using a simple graphic design software, Emerson worked and worked for hours, and I had no idea of what was coming about. And then when we saw what it was, we had it printed on nice paper, and it was so impressive. I loved the way she built this amazing project far beyond what was expected, and there was no one saying you have to work on your project. She was not someone who has had

an easy time at school. They were absolutely blown away, not only that she had done this without any help at all, the graphic design work and research, [but also because] it was fun to see her so passionate about something and really get into it.

During our conversation, Lucy asked Emerson to tell me about the difference for her between working on a team and working on her own. The answer revealed a curious aspect of Emerson's learning style:

> Working in a team for me is hard because I am always with the smart kids. Kids that are using all these weird fractions, and I am the one that always wants to do something out of the ordinary. Try something different, take chances. But no, everyone always wants to stick to the facts and deal with the "real." That's just not how I do it; I want to create something that is memorable. That is why I like to do it by myself, independent. I find it easier to work alone so I won't be judged or teased for my ideas. And I am not the boxed-in type of child. We are supposed to stay inside the lines. We are supposed to stay within the criteria, and with Genius Hour it was just fun to let my hair down and go at it.

PROJECT-BASED LEARNING SPREADS THROUGH CELEBRATION

Genius Hour is just one example of many approaches to project-based learning. They exist in all manner of ways, in school districts across the world. The magic of project-based learning, as we have seen from these examples, is they set the conditions for students to explore, through areas of interest, things that matter to them. Through our Lead the Way events, we profiled hundreds of such initiatives, because we understand that a critical condition for your own Wonder Walls and creative learning cultures is celebration, which we discuss in the next chapter.

Stories From the Field

Slam Poetry Is a Slam Dunk for Literacy Learning

The example of Morgan, a student, highlights how personalization—making learning meaningful for an individual—brings out the student's unique brilliance. Sometimes it just means providing students with the opportunity to do something novel or different.

Meggan Phelan, a teacher at Morgan's school, organized a slam poetry club, which was visited by a group of slam poets. After the poets talked about the genre and demonstrated their craft, they invited the students to take 15 minutes to write their own slam poems on a topic they felt strongly about. Each student then recited his or her poem to the group.

I was fortunate enough to be on hand that day to hear Morgan's slam poem. I was deeply moved by how she was able to put together such an inspiring poem in a short period of time. The content was clearly very meaningful and personalized to her, for she decided to express what it's like to live with autism in her slam poem. (Her poem, which follows, is untitled because, as she explained to me later, sometimes she doesn't get around to naming them!)

Untitled

I see a world different than you.

I see a world that gets upset if I scream when someone touches me.

I see a world that says things figuratively and gets upset when I don't understand what they mean, and it's not fair.

I live in a world that says I'm being difficult when I won't go in the cafeteria because it's too noisy.

I live in a world where people say that it doesn't matter if the freaking bowl is a different colour than the cup, even though it clearly matters and I can't eat dinner otherwise.

You see, you did it too.

I know it sounds strange that my foods can't touch and my pens have to stay in the right order.

But I am an autistic girl living in a neurotypical world and I know, believe me I know, it's hard to understand.

But maybe you could stop trying to find out what went wrong to make me this way and instead try to help.

Maybe you'll see we're not that different, you and me.

What also struck me about Morgan's poem was that it was not only a learning experience for her, but because it was personalized, it was a learning experience for us, giving us a glimpse into her world. So when I met with Morgan recently, I asked her to tell

(Continued)

(Continued)

me more about her experiences at school and how she had come up with the ideas and feelings expressed in her slam poem.

"I have difficulties dealing with noise, such as in a noisy classroom. It sort of overloads my brain, and the only thing I can concentrate on is the noise and I can't get the work done," Morgan explains. "Crowds in the cafeteria are also noisy so I usually eat in front of my locker or a teacher's classroom."

I asked her, "If you could design a setting that would maximize your chances of learning, what might that include?"

I think it would be neat if kids could get noise canceling headphones, because a lot of the time you need an IEP [individualized education program] for that. I think it could be helpful for all of the kids on the spectrum and indeed a lot of other kids who have trouble with noise. And I think in middle schools where you do not have the option to go and eat outside it could be interesting if there was a classroom designated as a quiet space. Because cafeterias tend to be stressful for me personally and a lot of people I know who don't have mental challenges and stuff.

Morgan also described how group work can be difficult for her. "A lot of the time people don't understand what I'm saying unless I specify it very clearly. I'm not the best at showing facial expressions in conversation and interpreting it. So it is harder for me to understand what group members mean and it's hard for me to see things from their point of view. I find that hard because I can't really get into the mind-set as well and understand why they would think that certain thing."

Morgan has found sketching to be another personal means to express her thoughts. "I did this one sketch to express my emotions at a time when I was going through a severe depression. I sketched a willow tree which was sort of bent and broken but the top branches were alive, the leaves falling off them, and they turned into teardrops at the end. I do stuff like that to sort of show what I'm dealing with. I'm able to say this is what I'm feeling because it's hard to express in words some of the things that go on in your mind. It's easier to show it in images. So I just sketch and draw and hang it up to see how I was feeling at that time."

Photo courtesy of Morgan McAteer

Try This!

Partnering Subjects: Increased Personalization and Increased Learning Outcomes

Positive and productive partnerships don't just take place outside the school; they can also take place within it. In *Spark: The Revolutionary New Science of Exercise and the Brain*, John J. Ratey (2008), an associate clinical professor of psychiatry at Harvard Medical School and an internationally recognized expert in neuropsychiatry, explains how pairing physical exercise with subjects such as math and language arts can improve outcomes dramatically—and appeal to students who may prefer phys ed.

As just one example, a Chicago high school that tried out the recommendations with a group of students with attention deficits saw the students' reading and comprehension scores increase by 50 percent over a control group—in just one semester. Moreover, the program has been shown to also dramatically increase attendance and improve disciplinary problems.

8

Condition #4: Celebrating

> *"People of our time are losing the power of celebration. Instead of celebrating we seek to be amused or entertained. Celebration is an active state, an act of expressing reverence or appreciation. Celebration is a confrontation, giving attention to the transcendent meaning of one's actions."*
>
> —Abraham Joshua Heschel (1975)

The examples you've seen throughout *The Wonder Wall* demonstrate how celebration—of our differences, common goals, challenges, and achievements—is pivotal to creativity. For Zita Cobb, it means tapping into the brilliance of each individual and the act of celebrating all facets of human capacity. It's the celebration of the furniture makers and the boat builders and the fishers and the oceanographers and how they have built the unique culture that is Fogo Island. For Anna-Karina Tabunar, it's the celebration of finding the gifts in people's abilities, rather than focusing on disabilities. For Dr. Martin Brokenleg, it's the celebration that comes from building a culture of belonging. And for Stephen Haff, celebration weaves through the beauty in literacy and life. They all, in their unique ways, created their own Wonder Walls.

One of the approaches we took from the beginning of our Lead the Way journey was to showcase creative initiatives at all our events. Because creativity is often ingrained as being confined to the arts, we wanted to model the idea that creative activity was a critical component in all human endeavors. We thus put out calls for creative examples from classrooms, our schools, the district departments, our partners, businesses, and the broader community—everyone we could possibly find.

We also thought Lead the Way events would be the perfect opportunity to build a community of belonging and to celebrate the creative work that our teachers and their students were doing. We knew there was all manner of creativity and innovation going on in the teaching of our students, and we were eager to showcase them at our upcoming event. We put out what we believe was a creative and inviting request for submissions, then we sat back and waited for the deluge.

A month later, we knew we were in trouble. Things had not gone as planned. With our Lead the Way event to showcase creativity looming a mere two weeks away, we had received only six submissions.

I was dumbfounded. We couldn't understand why this was the case, so I decided to check things out firsthand, because I knew there were a lot of creative initiatives out there. I got in my car and went on a tour of schools and departments. In the very first classroom I walked into, that of fifth-grade teacher Michael Wendler, I saw what is pictured below.

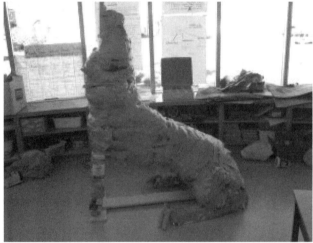

Photo courtesy of Michael Wendler

I wasn't sure whether I should proceed into the classroom or call for an exorcist.

Michael assured me that I need not fear, and the form emerging out of the classroom floor was, in fact, the embryonic stage of a life-size model of the school mascot: a griffin.

This immense work in progress was destined to be three months in the making. More than a symbol of school spirit, it was a symbol of communal and celebratory creative learning. Michael explained that he didn't start the project with a set of designs because he wanted the process to be an intricate part of the learning. So he posted pictures on his class website each day, inviting suggestions from students and parents alike as to how the griffin ought to take shape.

Michael was not afraid to tell his students or the parents the project would be somewhat of an experiment, as he wrote in his blog:

> We (mainly "I") don't really know what we are doing, but we are up for the challenge. The end product will hopefully be a paper mache creation that looks something like half-lion, half-eagle "ish" creature. But regardless of what the outcome is (no matter how monstrous), it should be a great learning experience . . . for all of us! :). We are looking for donations, if you have any of these things lying around the house . . .

As the project continued, Michael used it to pique the students' interest and spark their creative brilliance across academic subject matter.

"It needs a head. And wings. How should we make the wings? Anyone have any ideas?"

And along with the students' learning, the griffin took shape.

Until finally, there was nothing left for the students to do but to ensure their new griffin was well-fed . . .

And that was just my very first classroom. As I continued on through the day, I came across several fascinating projects being led by students and teachers, within the departments of the school district, with educational assistants, and parents. I immediately enrolled them in the conference.

Still, we were left scratching our heads. With such wonderful examples of creativity out there, I couldn't understand why more teachers and other staff members had not thought to send in their own submissions for the Lead the Way event. Was it that they didn't see these examples as creative? Were they shy or modest about sharing their fascinating ideas?

After discussing the matter with several staff members, the reason behind the underwhelming response became quickly clear. We were still defining what creativity was. We were also attempting a significant culture change. We were asking people to look at the things they were doing as works of creativity, and they weren't used to seeing their work that way. Moreover, the purpose of the Lead the Way events was still relatively new.

Photo courtesy of Michael Wendler

Photo courtesy of Michael Wendler

It was clear that going out into the school community to find examples and encourage participation directly was the right thing to do. Once we began sharing and celebrating examples of creativity, people began to understand what we meant and that we were serious about it. Just one year later, we again put out the same call for creativity submissions and examples, and this time we were inundated with nearly 250 remarkable, brilliant initiatives from all manner of different and diverse places: schools, classrooms, community partners, arts people, scientists, and more.

These celebrations of creativity became the highlights at our leadership and Lead the Way events. Participants from the schools and the broader community saw a student radio station; an Aboriginal community outreach initiative; a school culinary arts program; a nature reserve project coordinated by a community group; a house-building program, complete with students building a shed; and a student jewelry making business led by teachers and support staff of students with a variety of significant challenges, just to name a scant few.

There were also demonstrations of creative new ways of teaching, such as a pilot in which at-risk students participated in physical activity before a math lesson, with results that included not only higher marks but higher attendance ratings and better self-esteem.

We also invited creative examples and submissions from the broader community. One of these, for example, was Dr. John Bell. On August 31, 2011, news broke out of the Ottawa Health Research Institute (OHRI) of some groundbreaking research he was conducting in the field of therapeutic cancer viruses and their ability to attack and shrink tumors. The news was garnering national and international media attention, and no wonder—what an incredible example of creativity at work!

I decided to give Dr. Bell a call, on the very off chance he might be interested in profiling his amazing work at our next Lead the Way event. I wasn't that confident, considering how busy he must have been, but figured there was no harm in asking.

Given that I was calling on the day that the world's media was after him, I thought I would call and leave a voice mail explaining the context of the event. I wasn't expecting anyone to answer the phone, but someone did.

"Hello?"

I stammered in surprise. "Ahh. Yes. May I speak to Dr. Bell please?"

"Speaking."

"Excuse me?"

"This is John Bell."

"Oh. I'm sorry."

I explained to the doctor that the last thing I had expected was for him to answer his own phone, on what must have been an extraordinary day for him. I then explained who I was and the context of our creativity initiatives and Lead the Way and boldly asked if he might consider profiling his remarkable work at the event.

The doctor responded, "So let me make sure I understand this. Who are you with again?"

"The Ottawa-Carleton District School Board."

"Right. And your team is exploring ways to foster creativity through your classrooms and the organization and to demonstrate the importance of creative learning across different fields of human endeavor."

"That's correct."

"Well, that's most interesting," Dr. Bell responded. "I'd be delighted to have our work profiled. Just send me the details."

And with a few pleasantries, that was it. I couldn't believe it. I had just scored a presentation for our school board regarding the work of a man who was, on that day, one of the most talked about medical specialists in the world.

As I was to discover through the years, however, this would not be a one-time stroke of luck. It happened to us time and time again. The more we went out into the community, the more people learned about what we were trying to achieve, the more eager they were to become involved.

CELEBRATION ISN'T JUST AN EVENT, IT'S AN ATTITUDE

I learned two important lessons from Dr. Bell that day. The journey to creativity tends not to be linear; as more people get involved and add their ideas, and enthusiasm grows, the path begins to swirl upward, taking everyone up with it. I think it's because the core message is so profoundly optimistic, and inclusive, that it resonates with everyone. We have had no shortage of people, regardless of background, status, or time constraints, eager to join us. Once you get the word out there, especially if you take a strength-based, celebratory approach, you will be delighted at how many people want to help you and take part.

The second lesson I learned is that "celebration" isn't just an event, it's an attitude and a way of life. Our Lead the Way events were showcases to celebrate creativity initiatives, but the creativity actually began in the classroom, with the students and the teachers, and in our departments and the broader community across the district, with people like Dr. Bell.

It was that attitude of celebration, that sense of joy and novelty and the sheer *wonder* of learning and stretching the imagination, that really caused the life-size griffin to emerge out of the classroom floor and take shape—not the paper mache and other materials from which it was constructed.

For that reason, I consider celebration to be an integral and primary condition that must be present to support cultures of belonging, a strength-based perspective, and the Wonder Walls that bring out that seed of brilliance in every student that enhances their learning. And there are a number of ways to foster a sense of celebration in the learning environment.

In these times of complexity, however, I would emphasize that we need to bring more attitudes of celebration into our students' lives, our lives, and society in general, particularly when we are trying to build cultures of belonging and strength-based perspectives.

Dr. Martin Brokenleg, whom I introduced earlier, has an interesting perspective on this. "Because of the stresses of life, lots of people do not have experience in knowing how to celebrate and acknowledge those positive sides of life. When we grow up with stresses and adversity, we become fixated on the negative. With an attitude of celebration and a strength-based approach, you get out of that dysfunctional dynamic."

Moreover, Dr. Brokenleg says children and adults today may need to learn how to be happy:

> Back when I had a therapy practice, I would always keep several copies of a little book on my shelf by John Friel and Linda D. Friel [1990] called *An Adult Child's Guide to What's "Normal."* John Friel worked with people who had damaged family connections, and he discovered, which I did as well, that lots of people really have no idea how to express happiness. For example, they couldn't celebrate a birthday because they didn't know how people feel on their birthday. So the Friels wrote a chapter for each celebration or occasion, like Christmas or getting a promotion at work.

Because schools and work environments are places in which children and adults spend a large portion of their time, we have a tremendous opportunity to bring more joy and celebration into the world.

Stories From the Field

Celebrating the Magic in Math Class

Celebration involves novelty and enjoyment, and Al Overwijk, a teacher for 26 years, has seen the difference that making lessons more meaningful, enjoyable, and downright messy can have. Al has an amazing reputation as a mathematics teacher. Interestingly, his teaching methods underwent a massive transformation about a decade ago.

"I taught in a very traditional manner for the first 17 years of my career," he says. "It was very much the Socratic method: I'm going to show you how to work through a problem, then we'll try some problems together, then you'll do some, and here's your homework."

In retrospect, Al says he realizes this method of teaching took all the struggle away from students, "showing them a nice golden path of exactly what they needed to do to get an A-plus on the test. The students quietly absorbed what I taught and were valued for being able to replicate the procedures on the test."

This method worked very well while Al was teaching students in the academic stream, but when he was asked to teach an applied mathematics class, he realized he needed to change things.

As with the academic class, Al found he was most effectively reaching the top two-thirds of the class. But unlike the academic class, the students who didn't understand were not willing to sit quietly.

"That's what turned me around. These kids are jumping off the walls and they were not going to tolerate me not engaging with them."

Al finally went to the head of his math department and said he didn't think teaching the applied course was working out, for him or the students. Rather than giving up, the head offered Al the support he needed to try something different. The following semester, Al and the head each taught one applied course, working closely together:

> The first thing we had to do was to engage the kids. We decided to throw everything we know about teaching math out the window and just engage the kids in problem-solving and puzzle-type activities, to get them interested in doing math. We didn't worry about the content. The plan was to get kids active and get them engaged in the work.

The structure of the class also changed. Typically, math courses had been taught in a very linear manner: A unit's lessons on one subject, such as trigonometry, would move from easy to hard over a three-week period and then a test would be given before moving on to the next three-week unit on a different topic.

"We started to use the idea of a spiraling," says Al. "We created activities that encompassed multiple mathematical ideas and concepts in each spiral. We focused on making the task rich. We would spend maybe three weeks on that activity, but that activity would cover half of the big ideas in our course."

(Continued)

(Continued)

By combining the exploration of different ideas with spiraling, the same concepts were explored three or four times during a semester instead of only once, leading to more reinforcement for the students. And increasingly deeper understanding.

One activity from Al involves using bicycle rims to provide an experiential approach to trigonometry. Al went to bike shops, scrounged as many rims as he could, and deconstructed them. Then the fun began: a journey into the world of radians, arc lengths, angular velocity, and a host of other mathematical gems.

"This type of approach to teaching math is super messy because they have to figure it out themselves. That's very different from how I used to teach, with a very structured approach in which I told them to do this, then this," says Al. "The question is how do you make those magical moments happen for kids instead of telling them how to do it? That's the real challenge of a teacher, to orchestrate that magic."

You can learn more about Al's amazing world of math on his blog at slamdunkmath@blogspot.ca.

Photo courtesy of Al Overwijk

Learning is messy, Al Overwijk says. "Give them a problem they don't know how to find the solution to, and ask them to put the solution on the whiteboard. There will be crap everywhere. It won't be sequential, but that's not how mathematicians work, so why do we teach kids to do math that way? It's a matter of saying that didn't work, so let's try something different."

BUILD ON COMMUNITY PARTNERS TO FOSTER A SENSE OF CELEBRATION

As I've mentioned, building partnerships creates a wealth of new ideas and resources for creative learning. Partnerships are also valuable, though, in the way they enable students and teachers to be inspired, pushed, and informed by a variety of external sources. What better way to learn the science and biology behind organic gardening techniques than pairing up with a retirement home? What better way to see a math lesson in action, or learn about the trades and design, than inviting a construction company into your school and giving the students an assignment?

Even beyond these benefits, however, is the concept that connecting with other people is, in itself, something that brings joy, celebration, and feelings of community.

Through our Lead the Way events and other learning initiatives, we were able to form diverse and fascinating partnerships. These have included the following:

Local hospitals and health care organizations	The Rotman School of Management
Aboriginal partners	Queens University Business School
Local police	Other school districts
Scientists	The Ontario Ministry of Education
Arts organizations	The Provincial Government of British Columbia
The trades	
Universities and colleges	And many others

Partnerships also help form a sense of friendship and camaraderie as you share your successes, lessons learned, and ideas. In 2007, just a couple of years into our journey, I was contacted by Lawrence Alexander, who worked for Jessica McDonald, the deputy minister to the premier of British Columbia, who was in charge of the B.C. Public Service, some 2,700 miles away from where we were located.

As it turned out, Jessica was determined to foster a more creative and innovative culture throughout the province of British Columbia's Public Service. She had tasked Lawrence and others with formulating a plan, and he had come across our district's research and work on the Internet. They decided to contact us to pick our brains.

My creativity colleague, Frank Wiley, and I were invited to attend an event in Victoria, B.C., which would launch their creativity initiatives. In return, they wanted us to share our creativity journey with them and gain our perspectives on their plans.

This was the beginning of a fascinating two-year partnership in which we learned and shared with each other. What was especially valuable to me, once again, was the reinforcement that other people, from different spheres, were also interested in exploring leadership and creativity and the conditions under which the extraordinary can happen. They were trying to figure things out as they went along, just as we were, and the opportunity to share findings provided a wealth of learning. They were so dedicated to this culture shift that they took the time to come and present their ideas at our next leadership conference.

GOING ON A BUS TOUR: CELEBRATING CREATIVITY IN THE SCHOOL COMMUNITY

Learning from the response to our first call for submissions, we realized our students, teachers, and schools needed a better understanding of just what this whole creativity thing was all about. It was my comrade, Frank Wiley, who came up with the idea of a bus tour to help open up those doors and invite the school community to get involved, similar to the day I had set out and gone from school to school to find creative examples for our Lead the Way event. Except this time, we would have a bus, and whoever wanted to would join us, going from school to school and department to department.

We sent out an announcement for the bus tour that was tantalizingly brief: "We're going on a bus tour. Wanna come?"

The purpose of the bus tour was twofold. First, employees would be able to have an eye-opening opportunity to see what else was going on in other parts of the district, building awareness and understanding across the board. Second, external partners, who may have little opportunity to gain a deeper understanding of the realities of our world, could witness the complexities of education, thus boosting the potential for fostering real understanding and collaborative partnerships.

At the same time, we wanted to give a live demonstration of strength-based approaches in action. The various leadership teams involved in Lead the Way had become increasingly aware of and intrigued by this concept, which, as noted earlier, we had embedded into our own unique definition of creativity.

Strength-based perspectives flourish when developing collaborative relationships through positive questions. In the case of the bus tour, we gathered the participants the night before and introduced them to the concept of strength-based approaches. In essence, the entire bus tour became a strength-based event.

The bus tour was a resounding success. With an attitude of celebration, it brought together people from a broad spectrum of locations and sent them out to explore many locations they hadn't seen before. Together, participants were able to experience firsthand the excitement, the creativity, and the extraordinary in the everyday learning in the classrooms and other departments of our district. They saw people doing things in different ways and were invited to ask themselves, "What can I do to make things different? Special? Wonderful? Individual? Unique?"

CELEBRATING THE COMMUNITY WITH LEAD THE WAY EVENTS

Way back near the beginning of *The Wonder Wall*, I promised to give you a few examples of Lead the Way events. And as celebratory showcases for leadership and creativity, here we are.

Early on in our Lead the Way journey, we decided to model learning environments that reflected the types of creativity we wanted in our departments, schools, and classrooms. This grew from the premise that there is a seed of brilliance and creativity in everyone and that our imperative is to set in place the conditions and spaces in which it would flourish, re-creating the concept behind *The Wonder Wall*.

Elliot Eisner is a professor of art and education at the Stanford Graduate School of Education and one of the leading academic minds in North America. One of the ideas central to his thinking is the concept of forms of representation. He described how everyone has a unique way of representing his or her understanding.

For learning environments, this requires some flexibility for students to be able to explore and make sense of things in ways that make sense to them. Mathematicians express understanding by exploring the relationships between numbers, dancers through kinesthetic movement, musicians through the nuance of sound, and scientists through curiosity and the quest to answer "what if?" This is how they represent their understanding of the world. It's a deeply personal thing.

Eisner's (1998) ideas were important underpinnings of our events. If everyone learns in a different way and represents his or her understanding of the world in fundamentally different ways, then it is critical to recognize it, value it, and tap into it in order to celebrate everyone's learning. This celebration of the different ways of knowing underpins a culture of diversity and inclusivity.

We always started the planning for these events by doing thought experiments. We imagined what it would be like as people walked into the event. What would they see? Hear? Feel? Smell? Think? We needed their imaginations and senses to be captured from the outset.

We also partnered, as we were in the habit, with several local community groups to maximize our use of resources. In this way we were able to bring in world-renowned speakers for our events.

We also partnered with our students. Students from our culinary arts classes, for example, might prepare and serve magnificent canapes and finger foods to guests milling about before the event. They were so professional, and the food and presentation so delicious and creative, that community guests often could not believe they were students but assumed they were from a high-class catering company. This never failed to pump up the students, getting an opportunity to show off their hard work, hear praise for their creativity, and get real-life experience at a real event.

Working with this creative brilliance, it was celebration in action.

FLASH MOB: CELEBRATION OF CREATIVITY AND LEARNING

Following the publication of our 2012 report on the conditions of fostering creativity, we decided to further push our thinking around the findings. So we had a flash mob, of sorts. To be honest, I admit I didn't know what a flash mob actually was at the time, so it wasn't like the flash mob you would typically see. Still, the name stuck.

We wanted to hear reflections on creativity and our research findings from diverse perspectives, and so we invited four community leaders to join us. After giving their reflections and insight on the key aspects of our findings that resonated (or not!) with them, we had a short question period, and then the audience became the "flash mob," sharing their own perspectives with each other and the entire group by writing them down or through student volunteers capturing their ideas electronically.

To maintain our focus on the critical issue at the heart of this, which is the learning experiences of our students, about halfway through the evening a real flash mob broke out when 25 students from a local elementary school, who had crept into the proceedings all but unnoticed, broke into a dance that was a highlight of the evening.

The key points we learned that night helped spark several new ideas to enrich and inspire our thinking. Above all, the message we heard was that you must try to live and celebrate the conditions of creativity, rather than just talk about them, to foster a culture of learning that allows ideas to grow.

IDEAJAM

During a planning session for a story-sharing conference, one of the participants likened the emerging ideas of the event to musicians getting together to jam. He described how when that happens, the individuals all bring their own musical ideas and express them as best they can in the structure of collaborative music making. He then pointed out that this event was precisely the same, except the ideas were verbal instead of musical. And so was born the name and concept of the event called Ideajam.

Once the creative construct for Ideajam was established, the details fell into place very quickly. And because the concept was so novel, the structure that grew out of it turned out to be equally creative.

LEAD THE WAY TO FORMAL LEADERSHIP

This event focuses on providing information and networking for people who might be interested in pursuing positions of further responsibility. However, all employees are invited. In our panel presentations, we are careful to ensure representation of diverse perspectives.

On one occasion, we had a panel composed of a chief custodian, an educational assistant, a principal, and a vice principal, each providing their own five-minute perspectives on formal leadership. All four were compelling. The custodian, Luc, and the educational assistant, Kirk, told personal stories of how they had helped children with special needs and made their worlds a little better. Neither of them managed to get through their stories without breaking down, and taking the audience with them. There were few dry eyes in the room. We learned that sometimes celebration is expressed through tears.

A FOUR-ACT CONFERENCE

In our Lead the Way events, artistry was critical, whether we were looking at science or math or music or plumbing. We also used artistry to capture the ideas and gleanings of what we had learned and experienced. One of our high school principals, Richard King, has many talents as a leader, a musician, a sportsman, and an artist. For many years, he documented his interpretation of our events through art in different media—a great example of how artistry is used to capture meaning.

One such conference included a diverse range of our community. We wanted all the participants to actively engage, rather than simply be spectators, and for the content to be rich and interesting, with something practical that people could take away and use.

As Richard described it, "We wanted the structure of the conference to be as interesting as the content, so we set it up as a play in four acts. Our opening segment, or Act I, was about an hour long. We knew it was a bit risky, but we decided to do away with seats, save for those who needed to sit. We set up a space for 400 people, with two large stages on either side. It was a theatre inside a conference center.

"We then created an interactive multimedia event with video, sound, and music. A First Nations drumming group opened the event, making for a moving start. Our speakers, presenting a series of short and powerful segments, were staged around the room so that people had to turn and physically move to face the current action."

What followed was a series of very personal and poignant stories that touched on struggle, passion, resilience, sadness, and hope, covering the gamut of what we experience in our schools, classrooms, and society. One of the most moving stories, for example, was about a student who had been struck by a car and was not expected to live. His guidance counselor spoke about the experience and then showed a video of the young man today. This presentation reminded us that students can often bounce back from the deepest adversity. It was a true celebration of humanity.

CELEBRATE CREATIVE ENGAGEMENT: FIND YOUR VOICE, USE YOUR VOICE

Student Conference

In January 2015, the OCDSB took another step in the process of learning about imagination and creativity. We had always ensured that the student voice was a critical element in our Lead the Way events, but at this conference we focused exclusively on the perspective of the student. This was the students' opportunity to consider and share their beliefs about the best conditions for fostering healthy and creative individuals and environments.

The conference was formatted as a "students as researchers" conference, and the format itself was as creative as the subject matter. A segment of the conference was organized around an idea called "Speak Up in a Box." The questions posed included the following:

1. In what situations in school have you felt safe enough to express yourself?
   a. The importance of feeling comfortable
   b. The value of structured discussions
   c. Teacher excitement breeds student excitement

2. What does it look like when you are fully immersed in learning and creating something?
   a. Building a relaxed moment
   b. Getting in "the zone"

3. How do you learn best?
   a. Learning is active
   b. Making connections to the real world
   c. Adapting to student needs

4. What do you think is the connection between creativity and learning?
   a. When teachers are creative
   b. The gift of choice

Students were then asked to use their imagination and creativity to create a dream lesson plan. The ideas that emerged, once again, were extremely insightful.

These themes were very similar to those that emerged when we conducted our creativity study across the school community. We mapped the two sets of findings together and included them in a chart in the appendix of the study document.

INFUSING CELEBRATION IN LEARNING

Often, when I tell audiences there is a germ of brilliance in everyone and that we need to embed celebration in the classroom to foster our children's learning, people first get the impression I'm talking about self-esteem. They envision initiatives to tell all students they are generically special, to hand out sports trophies to all participants, to eliminate competition.

Ironically, although it was well-intentioned, the self-esteem movement only encouraged us to view children as more homogenous—everyone's a winner—and further hide or ignore an individual student's unique strengths and capacities. And because we can't make trophies for every skill, it means students come to view themselves through the reflection of those shiny trophies, rather than identifying and developing their own interests and brilliance and taking intrinsic joy, satisfaction, and celebration in that development.

As I stated, celebration is an attitude, not simply an event. There are many ways we can incorporate joy—and especially the joy of learning—in the classroom. We all need to laugh more. To experiment with the novel. To see mistakes as opportunities to learn. To make a mess. Admit when we don't know something. To invite others in and go out into the community. And most importantly, to build and feed our own griffins and make our own Wonder Walls.

⌐ Try This! ─────────────

Make a Collaborative Project Go Districtwide

Is there a project that your school board could do collaboratively to build a sense of belonging across the community? One of my favorite examples occurred at the OCDSB. Director of Education Barrie Hammond was well known as a leader who exemplified the district's 10 character attributes: integrity, respect, fairness, responsibility, perseverance, optimism, cooperation, empathy, acceptance, and appreciation.

When it came time for Barrie to retire, an idea was sparked for a collaborative, districtwide project to make a quilt based on those character traits, inspired by artist Esther Bryan's Quilt of Belonging. Students, teachers, custodians, managers, principals, receptionists, administrative assistants, and many others decorated more than 300 fabric leaves, which were then carefully stitched into a 16-foot fabric artwork created by Esther Bryan. Titled Growing Our Character, all 10 character attributes are represented in the roots of a tree, signifying that, as in real life, positive character traits take root and grow to become strong, powerful, and beautiful.

9

Assessing the Culture of Creativity

How to Get Buy-In and Fellow Travelers for Your Journey to the Extraordinary

"Everything that can be counted does not necessarily count; everything that counts cannot necessarily be counted."

—Albert Einstein

A s I mentioned in Chapter 1, the more things change, the more people feel an urge to control. This is an even more common reaction to change in times of complexity—not only in school boards but also in businesses and other organizations.

This approach works very well for a robotic assembly line or with sausage making. But again, people and students aren't standardized. We are unique by nature, and evolution has programmed that uniqueness right into our DNA—no two of us are exactly alike. Not even identical twins. And so we are making an uphill battle for ourselves when we try to make everyone conform. It may seem easier to do it that way, but in the long run, it stifles creativity and innovation because they, by their very nature, demand for things to be looked at and done differently.

But as I have mentioned some 22 times before in this book, every single person within an organization has ideas, knowledge, and talents to offer. That includes those who are adverse to change, or your ideas.

They also have valuable insight to offer, and you'd be remiss to ignore it simply because you may not agree with it. To create the conditions to foster creativity, you must include the insight of those people who don't want to follow your lead and address their concerns. And trust me, there will be those who don't want to follow your lead. For many people, the idea of letting creativity loose is a scary thing, something that will cause a loss of productivity at best and the chaos of trampling rainbow unicorns running amok at worst.

You'll find that even you are not immune to this fear. It happened to me. When I was involved with the Conference in Four Acts for the Lead the Way event I described earlier, I bolted awake one night in a cold sweat and decided I couldn't go through with it. What were we even thinking? Having no chairs? Setting up a professional leadership conference like a theater? It was too novel, too unorthodox, and too risky. What if it failed miserably? Better to be safe, I thought, and go with something more conventional.

I contacted my lead partner on the conference, Pino Buffone, the next day, and he fully agreed with me. Unfortunately for us, when Steve Massey, another member of our team, heard what we were planning, he took me to task. He pointed out that we were acting in defiance of our own teachings on creativity. We sheepishly had to agree, and I'm glad we did. We went on to have one of the most memorable and moving conferences ever.

So how do you get buy-in and enthusiasm for your shift in organizational culture?

First, as discussed previously, start by demystifying creativity. Assure others that creativity doesn't mean giving up all control and rigor. It means putting accountability into place, checking in as required, and letting people do what they need to do.

There isn't a one-size-fits-all solution to these challenges, but I have learned there are some pivotal characteristics required to foster a culture of creative learning: the sparking of curiosity; the collision of ideas; the challenging of assumptions; and, in this age of complexity, what is increasingly important, a challenge to the assumptions upon which assumptions are made.

There are three important practical strategies that emerge from this.

Strategy #1: Surround yourself with the most diverse group of people you can find.

- People from different cultural backgrounds
- People from a variety of educational, learning, and experiential backgrounds

- People from across all areas and job categories. Don't just look to the management and formal leaders, but reach out to people across the organization.
- People from outside your organization
- People who will look at things through a very different lens and provide totally different points of view
- People who agree with you
- People who don't agree with you

The beauty of inviting people who don't agree with you is that they may actually have a point that you do need to address, and including them will help them feel validated, more in control, and more enthusiastic to push the movement forward.

Strategy #2: Foster learning environments founded on trust. People will only engage fully if they truly believe their ideas are going to be taken seriously and they are not going to be judged for their ideas. A collaborative energy and a security of mutual respect and support are pivotal.

Strategy #3: Allow those who seek to control to create measurements to benchmark progress. People who seek to control are sometimes just as happy to be able to measure, assess, and analyze—and they will in fact serve an important purpose of seeing just what is working and what isn't, because this is an ongoing journey and things will always need to be examined and tweaked. Never undervalue those who seek to control or see them as a barrier or nuisance—they may have sound reason to object and their insight can help you come up with solutions that satisfy these requirements and make the whole initiative better.

One way you might measure and track progress in creativity is by gauging how your organization stacks up to the four criteria in the definition of creativity. Or take a look at the Assessing Conditions for Creative Learning checklist in this chapter and ask your students, teachers, or employees how often they see these activities in action and conditions in place.

START YOUR ENGINES

You're going to be driving down the road on an amazing, intriguing trip of a lifetime. Sometimes that drive will feel like you're in a TV commercial, driving a sports car on a mountainside with a clear view and the wind blowing in your hair (if you have hair). Other times, you're going to hit speed bumps or feel like you're stuck in traffic. Sometimes, you'll feel downright carsick.

And that's okay.

Don't expect your road to establishing the conditions for a creative environment to be an easy one. Despite all the benefits that creativity and innovation bring to individuals, companies, organizations, and communities—and no matter how much your top brass or team members say they want them—you will need to work with them and encourage them so you all make it to your destination.

DRIVEN BY FEAR

As mentioned, the main reason for reluctance is that some people find the idea of creativity and its foundational conditions to be scarier than the twins in *The Shining*.

Why and how this fear presents itself can differ from organization to organization, but here are some of the most likely fears you'll encounter and will need to coach people to overcome.

1. **Fear of the unknown.** What, exactly, is creativity? Your task, as a creativity leader, will be to demystify the concept. Like we did, you may need to lead your school district or organization on a quest to come up with your own definition, as well as to demonstrate how this cultural shift will bring benefits for all. Feel free to use our four-part definition of creativity, or come up with one that suits your unique needs. We'd love to hear what you come up with.

2. **Fear of losing control.** There is a strongly held myth that creativity can only emerge in a no-holds-barred environment, that rules, standards, objectives, rigor, and assessment are all at odds with creativity. Especially in older corporations, where environments are steeped in traditional culture, revered org charts, and rigid production processes, the idea of a creativity free-for-all can be especially disconcerting.

Your task will be to demonstrate over time that creativity can and does follow a process, has rigor, requires assessment, and rather than disrupting entrenched processes, helps them to expand and grow.

3. **Fear of losing autonomy or benefits.** Some fear that change will mean losing the power, prestige, influence, and salary they have rightfully earned. Those who followed the traditional rules of getting a prescribed education and then leaping up the steps of the corporate

ladder may feel threatened by flattened hierarchies or consider it unfair that leadership is now accepted from all levels of the company.

Your task will be to provide assurance that encouraging and supporting these new forms of leadership doesn't take anything away from the C-suite floor—it exponentially expands creativity and innovation that will benefit the company and all its members throughout, in a variety of ways.

4. **Fear of being left out or left behind.** This fear can present itself in two ways. First, there is the fear that one does not have any creative capabilities to offer or any talents that would be useful or valued by the larger group. With this fear, your task will be to create the conditions that will help draw out those talents and abilities, through fostering a culture of belonging and a strength-based approach.

The second way this fear can manifest is through a fear of diversity or a fear of rejection. As we explored earlier, past ages and trends usually favored certain skill sets or knowledge, a tactic that valued some groups while excluding others. Your task in managing this fear is to demonstrate that in the age of creativity, *all* viewpoints, knowledge, and experience are required at the table if we are to generate the most innovative and creative ideas. Creativity is the great leveler necessitating that every person is valued and welcomed equally. No one can be excluded.

5. **Fear of aimlessness and lost productivity.** Creative ideas, by their very nature, tend to be new, novel, and untested. How do you know where you're going with creativity? How do you assess creativity? What if an idea is put into action and then fails? And how do you know whether a creative environment will spawn innovation or simply lead to people wasting time or coming up with impractical ideas that can't or shouldn't be implemented?

These are questions that people in your organization might be thinking about. As a creativity leader, your task here will be to demonstrate, through examples such as those shown in this book, that fostering the conditions for creativity has far-reaching and beneficial impacts—far greater than you could ever achieve with the status quo.

As for assessing the merit of creative ideas themselves, that is a complex process that will depend on an organization's unique set of circumstances. That exercise is beyond the realm of this book, which is more about setting up the environmental conditions that allow creativity and innovation to flourish. Here, however, you can do much to assuage the fears of your colleagues by teaching and demonstrating that the conditions themselves are assessable and measurable and can be correlated with other company key performance indicators (KPIs).

There are two ways you can do this. First, encourage your organization to get into the habit of considering the conditions for creativity and how they're stacking up in your organization. You may want to organize a team, with representatives from all levels of the company and from the outside community, to meet monthly to assess and plan steps to fostering the conditions for creativity in your environment.

FORMALLY ASSESSING THE CONDITIONS FOR CREATIVITY

In addition, you can help overcome fears by giving those who need a formal way to assess your corporate changes exactly what they want. By formally surveying all levels of the organization and tracking the results, you will be able to demonstrate whether your company is fostering the conditions necessary to promote and support creativity.

Moreover, by comparing and analyzing these results year over year with other corporate KPIs, you may be able to track and demonstrate a correlation among your creative environment, productivity, new products and services, and the bottom line.

Such surveys will vary depending on the organization and its objectives, but each should ask specific questions about actions and their frequency that foster or support the creative conditions.

Here is one example. In terms of specifics, Sir Ken Robinson (2015) asked me what I might say to a school superintendent in the United States who was interested in imbuing their learning culture with a spirit of imagination and creativity.

Where do you start? How do you begin to shift the organization in the direction of creativity?

1. Take the temperature of your learning organization.

   Find out how people are feeling about the learning culture. Ask serious and thought-provoking questions.

   What are people's views on learning, leadership, and creativity?

   Where does imagination fit in the organization? On the individual, group, and organizational level?

What do people believe about leadership? The characteristics of ideal leaders? The behaviors of ideal leaders? And what are the consequences of different formal leadership styles?

Does the organizational culture foster informal leadership and personal creativity?

What is the organization doing to help or hinder individual, group, and organizational creativity?

Also ask how the current organizational learning structure is either supporting or inhibiting what you are doing. How could you improve?

Be prepared for honest answers. Tell people that you are sincere in wanting their real opinions. Make it intentional.

2. Use the information to take a strength-based approach to cultural change. Start this immediately.

Use the data to create a collaboratively designed vision or leadership narrative that captures the ideas that emerge from what you have learned. This collaborative model needs to be inclusive of employees from across employee groups. The hierarchies need to be flattened, and people need to see that this is the case. And as always, bring in people from the outside.

3. Put in place practices and structures that demonstrate to people you are listening to their ideas and responding from a strength-based perspective.

4. The conversation needs to be ongoing. Develop structures through which people's voices can be heard.

A culture of listening and storytelling is crucial. People will respond in different ways to this, so you need to provide multiple opportunities for input. Once people feel a genuine sense of belonging, then the learning culture ignites.

5. Tap into the power of partnerships.

Break down the barriers of your organization and bring in people from the outside. They will provide a totally different perspective. There are amazing transformational stories all around as businesses, municipalities, arts and science organizations, and a host of others try to figure out how to respond and operate in this new creative age. Seek them out. Invite them in. Visit them. Engage them in dialogue. Through this collision of ideas, this sparking of curiosity, you start to spark a dynamism.

Assessing Conditions for Creative Learning: A Checklist

To assess progress, it's helpful to consider reflective questions to guide thinking on each of the four conditions. Here are some examples of questions you might want to consider.

Condition #1: Storytelling and Listening

	Y	N
Do people have the opportunity to share stories, to share what matters to them?		
What does this look like for individuals?		
For groups?		
At the organizational level?		
Are stories shared from outside the organization?		
Do you encourage a culture of listening?		
Do individuals feel they have a voice?		
Do teams feel they are heard?		
Have you set up formal structures to ensure voices are heard?		
What does it look like?		
Are all voices heard?		
Is there equal opportunity across the organization?		
Does the culture foster curiosity and wonder for the individual, group, and organization?		
Do individuals and teams have the opportunity to think about and provide input on how things might be done differently?		
Do you encourage a culture that encourages people to challenge ideas or preconceived notions?		
Can you provide examples?		

Condition #2: Moving Beyond Diversity to Inclusivity

	Y	N
Do you engage diverse perspectives and points of view as an integral part of your decision-making and work culture?		
Is your organization culturally diverse?		

Do you engage a broad range of people with different thinking and learning styles?		
Do you engage the perspectives of people from across the organization?		
From a range of employee groups?		
Do you invite people in from other sectors and ask for their ideas?		
Do you take teams to visit other organizations?		
To learn about how they do things and how they think?		
If so, who do you take?		
Do you encourage the challenging of assumptions?		
Have you engaged your people in a dialogue around characteristics, behaviors, and consequences of leadership?		
Have you developed a narrative of leadership?		
Do you respect and value informal leadership?		
How?		
How is this lived in your organization?		

Condition #3: Making It Personal

	Y	N
Do you have an understanding of the interests and passions of the people in your organization?		
Do you have structures and processes that ensure you take these into consideration?		
Are individuals and groups excited about and engaged in their work?		
Do people look forward to coming to work each day?		
Is there a serious attempt to		
personalize work?		
define tasks collaboratively?		
set in place accountability and support structures?		
Do individuals and teams have autonomy to complete the task in their own way?		
Can you provide specific examples?		

(Continued)

(Continued)

Condition #4: Celebrating

	Y	N
Do you foster a culture of celebration?		
What does this look like?		
Who gets to celebrate?		
To what extent is there a culture of playful learning or experimentation?		
Do people play and interact with ideas and concepts in imaginative and creative ways?		
How is this encouraged?		
Do individuals feel comfortable in taking risks, to experiment with new and novel concepts and ways of learning?		
What are the safeguards in place to allow people to experiment while mitigating the risks?		
What are the consequences for failing?		
Do we say it's okay to experiment but react negatively when failure occurs?		
How do we handle experimentation that leads to success?		
How do we capture lessons learned from both negative and positive outcomes?		

MY LESSONS LEARNED

Looking back on my own journey to creativity, there are many things I know now that I wish I had known then. Again, although these may not be reflective of your particular journey, you may be able to glean some insight from my experiences, both good and bad.

1. You will need to comfort and reassure people at times.

What barriers can you expect to come up against? A partial list: autonomy versus anarchy, attachment to the status quo, the need to teach what creativity really is, top-down management, and overcoming the fears of people being displaced.

First, don't lie to yourself about how people really feel in your organization. Sometimes the truth hurts, but only by accepting it and admitting it can you begin to build the conditions that foster leadership and creativity.

Second, understand that people are threatened by change, and often the ones who feel the most threatened by creativity are the ones at the top, who have their own masters to answer to and accountabilities to address. Your job is to let them see the benefits of creativity and the rigor of the process.

Third, you must overcome the misperception that fostering creativity is at best a nice-to-have side dish at the annual employee conference and at worst a concept so at odds with business and productivity that allowing it will lead to chaos, anarchy, and ruin.

Great innovation often occurs during times of crisis, such as wartime, financial trouble, famine, hurricanes, and outbreaks of disease. Because during these times, you have nothing to lose. For example, these were developed for wartime use:

- Freeze drying
- Jerry cans
- Duct tape
- Microwave

What is challenging for schools and organizations is how to be creative when your back is not against the wall. How do you allow creativity to flourish when things are motoring along? When everything seems okay? The challenge is to find the sweet spot, so the organization, and the people in it, don't languish in mediocrity.

2. **Get your story of leadership out there.** Live it, and make it matter. Don't just talk about it, breathe life into it. The more people see demonstrable evidence of the good things your team is achieving, the more people will get over their fear and want to join in. Implement structures and points of interaction. Use celebratory events to engage people in what they have done. Stretch out into your surrounding communities and foreign communities, both literally and figuratively. Involve the media. Everyone loves a good news story. Get on social media and get a conversation going with people across the community.

3. **Form partnerships.** Bring the inside out and the outside in. Many people think about breaking down internal silos, which must be done, but also recognize your organization doesn't exist in a vacuum. Get out into the community and ask people about their ideas on leadership, creativity, innovation, and more. Invite local businesspeople,

students, children, stay-at-home parents, customers, and others to your staff meetings. Diversity is a key to innovation, and the age of creativity is the first age where no one should feel threatened or marginalized, because everyone is needed to contribute ideas. And sometimes those fearful of change respond better to outside validation than that from within the group.

4. **Get messy.** We sometimes talk about a creativity "journey," but this implies a beginning and an end. The creativity process is more circular, spiral, and constant; you must keep checking back, fine-tuning, and moving on again to ever-higher levels. It is more like a spiraling updraft than a journey. In other words, it's going to be messy, both literally and figuratively.

5. **Foster trust: Be a person of your word and, just as importantly, trust others by giving them autonomy.** There is a lot of mistrust in many organizations today. Consider the concept of telecommuting and flexible schedules. Whereas most executives believe employees working from home are less accountable, some studies show they are actually more productive than their office counterparts. Add in the benefits to the environment, infrastructure, organizational costs, and employee happiness and well-being, and you would think organizations and governments would be driving employees to telecommute when they can, even a day a week. But most don't—because they don't trust their employees to put in an honest day's work when unsupervised.

Although there has to be a degree of accountability, it needs to be strength-based. We can make people accountable, but let them have autonomy to decide how the work is to be done. Once direction is given and tasks guided, get out of people's way so they can make sense of work the way it makes sense to them.

6. **Encourage humor and play, experimentation, and the power of curiosity.** To bring out the feeling of flow and optimal learning, you need to let people enjoy the journey to creativity as well as their jobs. Encourage them to ask questions, such as can this be done a different way, what can be changed, what am I curious about?

7. **Provide assurance and encourage risk taking.** When we put on the *Jesus Christ Superstar* performance, we had no idea how it would turn out. We had many questions:
   - If we had kids who could play the roles
   - If any kids would audition

- If the church would let us do it (it was a Catholic school, after all)
- If we could garner the interest required to get support
- If we had the musicians who could play a score of this complexity
- If we would have a set
- How we could map out the scenes

One thing we knew we had was the incredibly diverse abilities of the students and the people around us, both within the school community and in the broader community. For those who may doubt you, or fear taking a risk, invite them to join you in finding solutions and exploring mitigation.

Remember, every person, every situation, every context, and the goals of every organization are different. I don't think any two paths to building and fostering creative capacity can ever be exactly the same. There's no magic bullet, and it won't always be easy. But it will always be worth it.

Stories From the Field

How Leadership Support Brings Out the Brilliance

When teachers Eleri Morgan, Sarah Forsyth, Tania Ovens, and Chris Hiltz heard about Genius Hour, they thought it would be a great way to bring project-based learning into their classrooms. Genius Hour, which is about allowing students to learn something of their choosing, resonated with the four teachers, in spite of the inherent risks they knew were involved.

Yet amazingly, they not only overcame the challenges with outstanding results with the students, they were also able to obtain the funding, resources and enthusiasm to expand the project across the district.

I met with these teachers to ask them how they had managed to do all of this, and in two words, the answer was "leadership support," particularly from their school principal, Jennifer Offord.

"We knew we were going to get questions and perhaps some pushback because we were breaking the mold a bit," says Eleri. "We needed to ensure we were still delivering what parents were expecting and it was grounded solidly in the ministry curriculum."

(Continued)

(Continued)

Here's a summary of just some of the ways Jennifer helped the team achieve their goals though her leadership:

- Jennifer trusted her teachers. Says Sarah, "Jennifer had faith we were supporting the children through the Genius Hour project-based learning initiatives and that we could make this magical experience work for the students."
- She let them know she trusted them. "Jennifer constantly told us 'I really believe in Genius Hour, and you guys are doing great things,'" says Eleri. "It was so important to have that encouragement as it reinforced our confidence."
- Jennifer helped facilitate support for Genius Hour. She looked for resources and connected with higher levels in the school board, and later the provincial ministry of education, to share ideas about the program to help people understand its value.
- She was proactive in providing essential professional development in creative and critical thinking to help the team frame the project. She brought in experts to help address how to link the project to critical-thinking skills and whether the project should be assessed. "This development helped us to create a roadmap from the projects to every learning skill," says Eleri. "The process was grounded in our own thinking, in a broader research base of learning and in the curriculum. We used this information when we designed our process and communicated our plans to the school, community, and parents. With the professional development leader, Garfield Gini-Newman, we were able to follow Jennifer's direction and then get his validation the direction was the right one. That reinforced that we were meeting the needs of both the children and the curriculum."
- Jennifer encouraged celebration of the project. She not only regularly checked in to see how the students were doing, but she also took on her own Genius Hour project and shared her challenges, mistakes, and successes with the students. She also demonstrated her conviction in the project by talking about it to other groups in the district. "She would come back from a principals' meeting and explain to us how she was describing Genius Hour to them," says Tania. "It let us know how important she thought it was, and that pushed us to achieve even more."

The teachers were pleased with the success of the program, but the greatest satisfaction came from watching the students thrive through Genius Hour.

"Many of the students who succeeded so brilliantly with the project had been students at risk," says Tania. "They were feeling good about the work, feeling good about themselves, and wanted to be at school, which for some of them was the first time in a long time they had felt like that."

Jennifer also supported an application for a grant proposal that the team was successful in receiving from the provincial Ministry of Education, one of only two for the district. Its purpose was to share some of the concepts learned about personalized learning through Genius Hour with teachers across the district. The team and their students subsequently presented at various Lead the Way events, and later the team was invited to present their work at the World Creativity Forum held in Oklahoma City.

When I asked Jennifer her thoughts on the experience, she said one of the highlights of her career was a remark by Chris Hiltz, in which he said one of the most important elements to the success of Genius Hour was the "yes culture" at the school, a characteristic she felt was a natural part of her leadership style and came easily in leading a school.

Try This!

Tell Us Your Experiences

Whether you're a student, teacher, a school employee, or a member of the community, we'd love to learn about your experiences and ideas regarding creativity and education. How do you feel about school? What did or do you excel in? Did you learn about your abilities only after you left school? What did you want to be when you grew up? Did anyone ever ask you? Did school encourage you or hinder you? What happened in the end? Please write to us at our website at www.petergamwell.com and let us know!

References

Bateson, G. (1972). *Steps to an ecology of mind: Collected essays in anthropology, psychiatry, evolution, and epistemology.* Chicago: University of Chicago Press.

Brendtro, L., Van Bockern, S., & Brokenleg, M. (1990). *Reclaiming youth at risk.* Bloomington, IL: Solution Tree Press.

Caine, M. (2011). *The elephant to Hollywood.* London: Hodder and Stoughton.

Capuzzi Simon, C. (2012, November 2). Major decisions. *New York Times.* Retrieved February 16, 2017, from http://www.nytimes.com/2012/11/04/education/edlife/choosing-one-college-major-out-of-hundreds.html.

Chase, C. (2015). *Creative by nature.* Retrieved February 16, 2017, from https://creativesystemsthinking.wordpress.com/2015/02/18/the-circle-of-courage-native-american-model-of-education.

Csíkszentmihályi, M. (1997). *Finding flow: The psychology of engagement with everyday life.* New York: Basic Books.

Dweck, C. (2006). *Mindset: The new psychology of success.* New York: Ballantine Books.

Eisner, E. (1985). Aesthetic modes of knowing. In E. Eisner (Ed.), *Learning and teaching the ways of knowing* (pp. 23–36). Chicago: University of Chicago Press.

Eisner, E. (1998). *The kind of schools we need.* Portsmouth, NH: Heinneman.

Friel, J., & Friel, L. D. (1990). *An adult child's guide to what's "normal."* Deerfield Beach, FL: Health Communications.

Gray, P. (2011). The decline of play and the rise of psychopathology in children and adolescents. *American Journal of Play, 3*(4), 443–463.

Heschel, A. (1975). *The wisdom of Heschel.* New York: Farrar, Straus and Giroux.

Hess, E. (2015, March). Is your six sigma stifling innovation? *InterBusiness Issues.* Retrieved February 16, 2017, from http://www.peoriamagazines.com/ibi/2015/mar/is-your-six-sigma-stifling-innovation.

Howe, N. (2015, July 15). Why millennials are texting more and talking less. *Forbes.* Retrieved February 3, 2017, from http://www.forbes.com/sites/neilhowe/2015/07/15/why-millennials-are-texting-more-and-talking-less/#721bacdc5576.

Jayson, S. (2013, July 18). Would you break up by sending a text? *USA Today.* Retrieved February 3, 2017, from http://www.usatoday.com/story/news/nation/2013/07/18/mobile-texting-breakups/2522933.

Langer, E. (1997). *The power of mindful learning.* Reading, MA: Addison-Wesley.

Lenhart, A. (2015, August 6). *Teens, technology and friendships.* PewResearchCenter. Retrieved February 3, 2017, from http://www.pewinternet.org/2015/08/06/teens-technology-and-friendships.

Muther, C. (2013). Instant gratification is making us perpetually impatient. *Boston Globe*. Retrieved February 16, 2017, from https://www.bostonglobe.com/life-style/style/2013/02/01/the-growing-culture-impatience-where-instant-gratification-makes-crave-more-instant-gratification/q8tWDNGeJB2mm45fQxtTQP/story.html.

Newport, F. (2014). *The new era of communication among Americans*. Gallup. Retrieved February 3, 2017, from http://www.gallup.com/poll/179288/new-era-communication-americans.aspx.

Ottawa-Carleton District School Board. (2006). *Leadership: A school district initiative*. Ottawa, Ontario, Canada: Author.

Ottawa-Carleton District School Board. (2012). *Unleashing potential, harnessing possibilities: An odyssey of creativity, innovation, & critical thinking*. Ottawa, Ontario, Canada: Author.

Paul, A. M. (2012, March 17). Your brain on fiction. *New York Times*. Retrieved February 16, 2017, from http://www.nytimes.com/2012/03/18/opinion/sunday/the-neuroscience-of-your-brain-on-fiction.html.

Pink, D. (2009). *Drive: The surprising truth about what motivates us*. New York: Penguin.

Ratey, J. J. (2008). *Spark: The revolutionary new science of exercise and the brain*. New York: Little, Brown.

Robinson, K. (2011). *Out of our minds: Learning to be creative*. Chichester, UK: Capstone.

Robinson, K. (2015). *Creative schools: The grassroots revolution that's transforming education*. New York: Viking.

Schumacher, E. F. (1978). *A guide for the perplexed*. New York: Harper & Row.

Sirman, R. (2009, April). *The fallacy of the right answer*. Speech to the Ottawa-Carleton District School Board, Ottawa, Ontario, Canada.

Swanbrow, D. (2010). *Empathy: College students don't have as much as they used to*. Ann Arbor: University of Michigan. Retrieved February 3, 2017, from http://ns.umich.edu/new/releases/7724-empathy-college-students-don-t-have-as-much-as-they-used-to.

Wheatley, M. (1992). *Leadership and the new science: Discovering order in a chaotic world*. San Francisco: Berrett-Koehler.

White, M. C. (2013, November 10). The real reason new college grads can't get hired. *Time*. Retrieved February 16, 2017, from http://business.time.com/2013/11/10/the-real-reason-new-college-grads-cant-get-hired.

Index